Bruce Robinson

BEHIND
THE
TEARS

Understanding,
surviving & growing
from suffering.

Dr Bruce Robinson

Robinson, Bruce (author)
BEHIND THE TEARS
ISBN 978-1-922803-19-1 (paperback)

Typesetting Calluna Light 10/16
Cover and book design by Green Hill Publishing

Dedication

This book is dedicated to the most important people in my life, my lovely wife Jacqui, my children Simon, Scott and Amy, their partners Pip, Kate and Kyle and my grandchildren Olivia, Chelsea, Spencer, Darcey, Isaac and Mimi.

This book is also dedicated to Twink Parry who roughly sketched a map for me on a scrap of paper in northern Thailand which changed my life (see Chapter 1).

Contents

Acknowledgements

I wish to thank the many who have contributed quotes and ideas to this book. A special thanks to Bryan and Twink Parry, whose story appears in chapter two. Also to Mark and Darlene Zschech, who strongly encouraged me to put my thoughts into a book, as well as the many who kindly reviewed the text and made helpful suggestions. I owe a major debt to Owen Salter for his brilliant editorial assistance. I also wish to thank Phillippa Robinson for helping with typing the manuscript. My beautiful family, as always, has been wonderfully supportive of my efforts to use my experience to help others.

Preface

It is commonly felt that we don't do well at understanding and handling suffering or responding to those who suffer. We want to, but we often feel inadequate. I felt that so often when I was young. This book is written both to help you deal with your own suffering and to help you help others who are suffering or caring for sufferers. It also aims to develop and strengthen faith because suffering is one of the biggest challenges to belief in God.

Anybody reading this book is likely to have experienced suffering at some level. I say that because my deepest emotion when talking about suffering is that of weeping with those who weep. If you are reading this book and have suffered, I begin by expressing my compassion towards you. Please understand this as you read the book.

I am often asked to talk about suffering, particularly by Christians, because of my extensive experience of it in its deepest and most visceral forms. I have seen it as a doctor working in areas of massive hardship and destruction after natural disasters, and I have seen it in my role of breaking the bad news to patients that they have cancer and then walking the journey with them as they die. It is impossible to tell a young mother with children she has terminal cancer or to care for an innocent young boy who has lost his entire family in a tsunami without confronting the issue of God and suffering.

I get asked the same three questions again and again by those who suffer, regardless of their level of faith:
- Why is this suffering happening?
- How can I handle it when I am feeling sad and crushed?
- How does the Bible's promise of 'growth' from suffering happen when I don't feel like it is?

This book will help you think through these questions. I also hope it will help you grow and better express your compassion towards others in ways that are helpful and not hurtful.

How this book differs from other books on suffering

I was initially reluctant to write this book because there are already many good books on suffering. I have read a lot of them. But several Christians whose opinion I respect felt strongly that my personal 40-year experience of dealing with those who suffer, in the most horrendous of circumstances, gives me a special voice of authenticity. They also said that I talk about suffering in a way that is extremely useful because I discuss strategies that have proven helpful.

That is because my approach is largely practical. This book is not primarily a theological or philosophical study of the issue of suffering—there are other excellent books that focus on that, and they are listed under Resources. Rather, I focus on how we can understand, survive and grow from suffering in its different forms. I highlight personal experiences of the worst sorts of suffering so that readers can feel and think about the topic from the heart, not just the head. By concentrating on the existential nature of suffering and our response to it, I hope to move readers to greater levels of compassion and action—that is, closer to the way Jesus responded to suffering.

In short, this book fills an important gap in the repertoire of Christian books about suffering. It is a book for every person who suffers or who encounters people who suffer, either in the church or in the wider community, to equip them to respond with the compassion of Jesus and be a sweet aroma to those who are hurting.

Throughout the book I share personal stories, both my own and others'. I do this for several reasons:

- These experiences are suffering seen up close, and thus they enable the reader to 'enter into' the suffering of others. That is vital because it is what God did for us—entering into our world and suffering with us—and it helps us to be more heart-oriented towards the issues, more Jesus-like. This is not just an intellectual exercise.

- The presentation of ideas, tips and strategies from people who have understood and responded to their suffering as individuals, families, churches or other communities has been helpful to others. I find that everyone is looking for helpful tips.

- The honest disclosure of personal journeys of pain, sadness and anxiety encourages others to express their own feelings of sadness, anger and disappointment without feeling a need to 'pretend'. This is a big challenge in church communities.

- Sharing stories shows that seeing horrendous suffering is not an automatic knock-down argument against Christianity. Knowing that I have seen so much terrible suffering up close yet remain a committed Christian has proven to be encouraging both for people of faith and for those exploring faith. It becomes impossible to declare that 'everyone who has seen deep suffering stops believing in God'.

Christians use the Bible for direction, like a car GPS in an unfamiliar city. In this book I use Bible verses extensively. I also quote from other individuals who have suffered and/or who work with those who suffer because they are a rich source of wisdom on how to survive and grow from suffering. God expects us to learn from these individuals as well.

One of the main ways we move from abstract knowledge about God to a personal encounter with him as a living reality is through the furnace of affliction.
Tim Keller

Throughout the book you will find 'huggy-friend' boxes like this. These are intended to recognise, with compassion, how hard the question of suffering is and to express empathy for the likely suffering you will have experienced. It is very important to me that you understand this. This book is not a simple, quick answer to the agonising questions people have about suffering, nor is it designed to convince people that God exists despite the presence of suffering in the world. I appreciate that even trying to do that can sound dryly intellectual to those who are suffering right now. It can seem lacking in empathy—seeing so much suffering at the coalface has taught me that. I honestly want to send you these hugs.

PART 1

Understanding
Suffering

CHAPTER 1

Why understanding suffering is important for everyone

A young man left the church because all he heard from other Christians was that his questioning about suffering revealed a lack of faith. But he felt that blind faith was inadequate to understand big issues like the suffering he had seen.

The purpose of this chapter is to help readers understand that suffering is common and often hidden. We all need to understand suffering—for our own sakes if we suffer, to become more helpful to others who suffer, and to answer the challenges that young Christians and those without faith encounter with the issue of suffering.

Earthquakes, coronavirus, terrorist attacks—hardly a month goes by when we don't have to deal with one or another form of suffering. We experience it as communities, families, individuals. We watch it on the TV news. Then someone we care about gets told they have cancer and will die, bringing us to tears. And all around us are thousands of individuals suffering in silence with depression, chronic pain and deep disillusionment, too afraid to reveal their suffering to others.

Being human has always included experiencing suffering. We all end up with physical and emotional scars, and every scar tells a story. God made it possible for that to happen. This fact has caused many to be angry at God or to refuse to contemplate faith because of the presence of suffering in the world. 'Even if God made the world,' they say, 'he must be capriciously unloving to allow for the imperfections that permit the sadness, pain, suffering, grief, depression and death we all experience.'

Suffering is common

A good place to start thinking about suffering is to understand the sheer amount of it in the world. We can pretend that suffering is not all around us and that we don't need to think about it, but that doesn't help anyone.

Suffering is everywhere. Each year worldwide over 60,000 people die from natural disasters, over nine million die from cancer and over 20,000 die from terrorism. Annually there are more than 400,000 murders and 250,000 rapes. Every day around 20% of individuals including pastors) battle mental illness and 45% of adults struggle with chronic conditions. Suffering is inescapable, and we are all at times participants in this world of despair.

> *The kingdom of suffering is a democracy, and we all stand in it or alongside it with nothing but our naked humanity.*
> *Phillip Yancey[1]*

We suffer privately. We suffer together when a member of a school, church, workplace or extended family gets hit with something tragic. We suffer collectively during massive tragedies such as the COVID-19 pandemic, Hurricane Katrina, the Bali terrorist bombings, 9/11 and the Japanese and Indian Ocean tsunamis. Suffering touches us all and deeply affects us—physically, emotionally and definitely spiritually.

Suffering is a great equalizer. When I look at any family or other group of people, I assume they have all experienced, or are experiencing, suffering in some form. It may not show, but it will be there. Knowing that makes me more aware of the need to think about it and be ready to respond. We *all* need to think about it or risk responding poorly to our own suffering and that of others.

> **WE CAN PRETEND THAT SUFFERING IS NOT ALL AROUND US, BUT THAT DOESN'T HELP ANYONE**

Some suffering is obvious, but much is hidden

Much of the suffering that characterises human existence is all too obvious. Historically it has included world wars, tuberculosis, smallpox, the expected death of half of the children born and the pillaging, mass rape and enslavement inflicted by marauding tribes. Public suffering continues today in different ways. The COVID-19 pandemic, for example, has killed millions. As I write, my clinical department is at the front line, being a pulmonary department, and colleagues elsewhere have nearly been crushed by this disease. Every country has suffered, not just from the illness itself and the deaths it has caused but from the fear of it, the panic, and the loss of jobs, financial security and social contact. The vaccines are working, but regardless, there will be another COVID-19-like pandemic at some stage in the future.

Natural disasters always hit the front pages of the newspapers. A 'natural' disaster is a non-man-made event such as a flood, earthquake, hurricane, tsunami, tornado or volcanic eruption that causes great damage or loss of life. Natural disasters are sometimes called 'acts of God'. Devastating earthquakes and tsunamis in my region of the world, especially Indonesia, leave poor families weeping over the loss of their homes, their children, their livelihoods.

Most of the time, however, physical natural disasters occur at a distance from us, so the human suffering caused doesn't affect us so deeply. Our family or friends may see such events as arguments against God, but they don't touch us or our communities like other more personal forms of suffering. Many of these personal forms of suffering are hidden. Some of them are more common today than in the past. Each one has different impacts on the sufferers and those around them. I have noticed as a doctor that if you 'scratch the surface' of anyone older than around 35, you will find grief, often caused by one or more of these hidden types of suffering.

Examples of suffering that are often hidden

We won't be able to help others if we don't understand these hidden types of suffering, and we won't be able to handle our own suffering unless we acknowledge and deal with them. This is especially important because those whose suffering is hidden often feel shame or believe that they are frauds.

Why it is necessary to understand suffering

Understanding suffering is equally important for those who suffer, those who care for sufferers and those for whom suffering is a challenge to faith.

Understanding more about suffering is helpful for those who suffer. The first question I am usually asked by a sufferer is *why?* Why me? Why my child? Why does God allow it? Why does my family also have to suffer? Why now, when I have so much to do?

The Bible makes it clear that suffering is unavoidable. Anyone who has read Psalm 23 knows about the valley of the shadow of death, that dark, fearful place that God tells us we will all enter at some time, to some extent. You may feel you are in the valley of the shadow of death now, and if so, I hope and pray you will find this book helpful.

The Valley of the Shadow of Death (Psalm 23) represents an unavoidable experience for everyone at some time

The Bible does have some clear answers to the issue of suffering and ways to respond to it. But it also declares that we can only see these things through a mist—through 'a glass darkly'. What the Bible does provide is a roadmap for the future. It also makes clear how we can get through the valley.

Understanding more about suffering is helpful for those who care for sufferers. We see someone suffering and feel an urge to respond. But it can be hard to know what to do. Typically, when we care for someone who is suffering, *we* feel frustration and sadness too, but we don't know how to express those feelings. Consequently we can say or do we feel compassion, but we find ourselves saying or doing things that make matters worse. Or we are so afraid we will say something unhelpful that we say nothing at all and end up avoiding the suffering person.

We may hesitate because we are fearful of making matters worse. Sometimes we do nothing—not because we don't care, but because we feel out of our depth.
Sally Sims[2]

I have cared for many hundreds of cancer patients; I have seen poverty, disease and sadness in countries like Nepal, Papua New Guinea, India, Bangladesh and Afghanistan; and I have worked as a medical volunteer in some of the worst natural disasters in modern memory.—I have wept with people in each of those settings. It has been impossible for all of that not to touch my heart and drive me to learn more about people's suffering. I now feel it is an honour to be present in such moments.

Most of us don't feel comfortable talking with people who are suffering about what they are going through. It takes an effort to learn what to say and how to say it, plus what *not* to say. This book will help anyone willing to make that effort.

Understanding suffering is helpful for developing and defending faith. Suffering is one of the greatest challenges facing Christian belief, and a confronting issue for those interested in faith. So it is crucial to be able to understand and discuss it. Avoiding such discussions can lead to disillusionment with the church and to disbelief. Rather than using clichés to sidestep the issue, we need to face it squarely and honestly. Without that, we risk alienating those Christians, or children of Christians, who watch the TV news or experience suffering themselves and want answers.

Why failing to discuss suffering is so damaging

Failing to discuss suffering and similar difficult issues can challenge the faith of Christians. Here is the personal story of one such young Christian who became spiritually disabled, confused and disillusioned by the failure of the church to address questions such as 'Why is there human suffering?'—and what happened when he found people who did address them with an open mind.

THE STORY OF 'TWINK'S MAP'

Bryan and Twink Parry and their children in Thailand

In the mid-1970s, Dr Bryan Parry, his wife Twink and their three children were working in a mission hospital in Manoram, central Thailand. They had the sort of commitment that would take a whole family away from their comfort zone to work with the poor to ease their suffering. Bryan was a surgeon. The work was busy.

A disillusioned visitor

While they were there, they were visited by a long-haired, bearded backpacker in faded jeans. He was traveling through Asia on a journey of 'self-discovery'. He told them that although he had been a Christian for six years, he had become disillusioned by what he saw as the church's failure to engage with key questions posed by himself and his friends—questions such as 'How can a loving God allow suffering?' When people suffered, he said, they were told, 'It will all be OK in heaven, so just pray for patience'; 'Everyone can be healed if they have enough faith'; 'Suffering is all due to Original Sin and the fallen world.' They even heard that 'all sufferers deserve whatever they are going through'—a notion indistinguishable from primitive superstition. He said he felt that blind faith alone was never enough to understand this life.

Freedom to search for answers

Being told that it was 'better to show more faith and pray more' was enough to create disillusionment. So he had decided to put his career on hold, leave home and start thinking and living free of dogmatic and interpersonal constraints. He began to travel the world, searching for an authentic truth chosen by questioning and open-minded consideration rather than tribal dogma. By the time he left for his trip he had dropped his faith and was reading 'God is dead' literature. He happened to visit the hospital in Thailand where the Parrys were working.

During an evening meal with Bryan and Twink, their empathy must have made him feel listened to, because that conversation unearthed his concerns and his smouldering anger and frustration, emotions he often kept hidden in Christian circles for fear of losing acceptance. They listened to what he had to say and then in response suggested that the best place for him to go was a Christian community they had stayed at in Switzerland known as L'Abri. After the meal, Twink drew a small 'mud map' on a scrap of paper to help him locate it in the Swiss Alps, because it was hard to find.

The young man continued his backpacking trip and ended up in England. For some time he kept on with his personal search. But two years later, after several months backpacking around Europe, he finally remembered Twink's mud map, buried at the bottom of one of the pockets of his backpack. Using that two-year-old map, he eventually reached L'Abri.

Honest answers to honest questions

His time at L'Abri changed his life. He entered the commune as a disillusioned, questioning young man, the very sort of person the community was established for. He spent his days working, studying, discussing and arguing. He listened to thoughtful Christians dealing with complex issues like human suffering, especially the founder, Dr Francis Schaeffer. Questions were encouraged, and he thrived. He left with the feeling that although Christianity was not crystal clear on some issues, it stood on a rational, reasonable foundation, whether considered from a philosophical, psychological, sociological, historical or biological perspective.

Because of this experience, the young man's Christian faith was restored—more thoughtful, more authentic, more personal and more solid. All of this underpinned and changed the way he lived his professional and personal life from then on. He had moved from myth and dogma to a position of personal life-changing conviction, and a sense that issues like suffering could be examined thoughtfully and rationally. And all of this was in large part due to Bryan and Twink's encouragement, and Twink's mud map.

Twink Parry with the two children who were killed in Thailand

Two years after sketching that map on a scrap of paper on their kitchen table, Twink Parry and her children headed out from the hospital with other team members for a Saturday picnic. Bryan stayed behind because he was on call for emergencies. A truck smashed into their bus, instantly killing Twink, her daughters Becky, 5, and Adele, 2, and nine others. Bryan was devastated. It is hard to imagine the level of suffering he felt.

Their sacrifice and suffering have since inspired many. Certainly the life of at least one young backpacker was forever changed partly as a consequence of their willingness to discuss difficult issues and offer encouraging advice. When I heard about that bus accident and the deaths of Twink and the girls, I felt terribly sad. And I am weeping now as I write this story, because, if you haven't guessed already, that young backpacker was me.

Understanding how people respond to evil and suffering

Everyone reacts to suffering in different ways. Knowing this is helpful because it will inform how we answer the 'why' question. In the end, our responses to suffering are an individual choice, with some of those responses being easier or harder to embrace depending on our individual history and personality.

I was reminded of this diversity of response while working as a young man on a relief team following Cyclone Tracy, which ripped through the northern Australian town of Darwin on Christmas Eve 1974. Most of the town was destroyed, so children woke to devastation, not Christmas gifts. One father I spoke to had gathered his family during the cyclone in the only brick section of their home, the bathroom and laundry downstairs, and the storm destroyed the entire house except for where they were sheltering. He prayed throughout the night and gave thanks to God in the morning when they survived. Another man had been staying at the YMCA; watching the window of his room bending in and out he knew that at any moment it would explode and shower him with glass, so he pulled the wardrobe out from the wall and sheltered behind it. Sure enough, the window did explode, and jagged glass and raging winds burst into the room. He told me he shook his fist at God and shouted and swore at him over the noise of the storm.

The same event but two completely different reactions. Ultimately, we choose to think about suffering in ways that are driven by our emotions more than our logic. The great scientist Charles Darwin was a Christian until his beloved ten-year-old daughter, Annie, died. This sequence is common. How we view suffering is also driven by our community, that is, by people whose thinking and actions we like and admire.

I would argue that a considered, thoughtful view of suffering is more likely to be a strong foundation for the future, for dealing with our own and others' suffering, than a visceral, purely emotional view. Yet there will always be a 'heart reason' behind people's interpretation of their suffering, and it is helpful to find out what that is—to understand suffering from 'behind the tears'.

> WHAT DOESN'T KILL YOU CAN MAKE
> YOU STRONGER, BUT IT CAN ALSO MAKE
> YOU WEAKER... IT'S YOUR CHOICE

Understanding suffering can transform the future

One thing is clear from the Bible—suffering is not meant to leave us in a valley of despair but to transform us, to make us better people. This is not only a clear biblical mandate but has also been observed by many who have suffered or witnessed suffering.

> *And the God of all grace, who called you to his eternal glory*
> *in Christ, after you have suffered a little while, will himself*
> *restore you and make you strong, firm and steadfast.*
> *1 Peter 5:10*

> *Scars are tattoos with better stories.*
> *Anonymous*

Suffering can transform your future, but this might be for good or bad. If suffering is not dealt with, it can lead to blame and bitterness. It is not true that 'what doesn't kill you makes you stronger'—it *can* make you stronger, but it can also weaken you and leave you stuck in the prison of grief and despair. Responding well to suffering includes seeing it as a foundation for looking forward and answering the 'what's ahead of me?' question: 'How am I being transformed?' Not doing this has left many individuals stuck in the valley, either depressed and frustrated or locked in anger and bitterness.

> *We also glory in our sufferings, because we know that suffering produces perseverance; perseverance, character; and character, hope.*
> Romans 5:3

How this book may help

It might seem morose to talk about all of this suffering, but I think it can drive the opposite outcome. It can help create emotionally rich, compassionate communities of people who are growing in wisdom and communication skills, people who respond to their own and others' suffering with confidence instead of fear. Churches can be these kinds of communities. That is why I believe that all church members should learn the kinds of skills described in this book, and why every pastor, carer and friend should have a well-used copy of a book like this on their desk. Teaching parishioners and other groups to respond better to suffering is important for

- their parish—to teach their church about being prepared to handle suffering and respond appropriately to it
- their pastor—because a pastor's job is hard, and suffering is common in their profession

- their wider community—to enable Christians to better express the love of Jesus in their neighbourhoods, workplaces and schools.

I appreciate that in reading this book you might remember and even relive some of the suffering, pain, frustration, sadness and hurt that you or someone you care about has experienced and may still be experiencing. I am sorry if this happens. I acknowledge too the anger you may have felt towards God and towards the world and others, and that this may have led you to massive doubts about God's existence or his love, and may even have caused you to lose your faith. I hope you will find something in this book that helps you on your journey. And if you know anyone who is struggling with suffering, as either a victim or a carer, you might consider making a time to discuss parts of this book with them over coffee.

Key points

- Everybody will suffer at some time—it's part of being human and alive.
- People suffer in a wide variety of ways today, many of them hidden.
- During times of suffering the anguish can feel crushing and inescapable.
- Friends and family often don't know what to say to sufferers, and their words and actions can make things worse. We all need to get better at it.
- A deeper understanding of suffering is valuable to both those who suffer and their carers.
- Suffering can transform our futures, for good or bad.

CHAPTER 2

Why suffering happens

'SHE DIDN'T DESERVE THIS': Emotional tribute to Perth woman as accused murderer faces court. Her sister says the 55-year-old was loved dearly and did not deserve to be killed.
Newspaper report

The purpose of this chapter is to clarify how Christianity understands suffering. Not all Christians understand it the same way, and many don't understand the biblical view at all. It is only in understanding that view accurately that we can think it through clearly. The chapter finishes with a summary of non-Christian views to add perspective.

'Why is there such awful suffering in peoples' lives?' is one of the commonest questions I get as a Christian who has seen the worst of sickness and tragedy. I think this is the biggest challenge for atheists and believers alike. It is the question likely to make Christian apologists squirm in their seats as one horror story of misery and heartache after another is recounted.

Perhaps you have asked yourself that question too.

Getting answers to the question of human suffering requires a lot of honesty. It also requires openness and study of what God really says. Without that we risk disillusionment and confusion. The Christian view of suffering is not only helpful but also a logical, reasonable response to the issue. It is quite different to the views of other religions and atheism. The Christian understanding can be both an entry point to deciding what is true about suffering and a potential comfort and roadmap to a better future.

> **THE CHRISTIAN VIEW OF SUFFERING IS HELPFUL,
> LOGICAL AND REASONABLE**

Why do innocent people suffer?

Natural disasters are an ideal way to think again about suffering because there is usually no question about the innocence of the victims. They haven't smoked and contracted lung cancer; they haven't been drink-driving and crashed into a tree. And the victims are often children, which tears at the heartstrings.

Coastal town smashed by the 2004 Indian Ocean tsunami

As a sad, visceral example, here is something that happened to an innocent 12-year-old during the Indian Ocean tsunami in 2004.

INNOCENT CHILDREN PLAYING SOCCER

At 8 am on a bright sunny Sunday, the day after Christmas, a large tectonic plate shifted off the coast of the northern Indonesian island of Sumatra. It produced a surge of energy more than a thousand times greater than the Hiroshima atomic bomb, sending a pressure wave through the water towards the unsuspecting citizens of the Sumatran province of Aceh. It crossed the ocean at the speed of jet plane, slowed as it approached the shallow waters of the coast and then rose to frightening heights as thunderous 25-metre waves that smashed into unsuspecting communities along the shoreline.

The town closest to the epicentre was Meulaboh, so it was the first town hit, 15 minutes after the earthquake. The tsunami destroyed everything in its path and swept tens of thousands of shocked, frightened citizens away to their deaths. The wave then struck the rest of Aceh and crossed the Indian Ocean to kill many thousands more, especially in Thailand, Sri Lanka and India.

In Meulaboh a 12-year-old boy named Mo lived with his family near the sea. I met him when he visited our medical tent during one of our post-tsunami clinics. He came to eat our lunch 'leftovers', though in reality our cook always made sure there was enough food to keep him nourished.

On that fateful Sunday morning he had been playing soccer with agroup of friends in a field near the ocean. The first large waves came ashore, flooded the field and frightened them. They weren't to know what terror would happen next. Several more waves, much larger, thundered towards them, and because they were on a peninsula, the waves came at them from

Mo, an innocent child victim of the tsunami

three sides. Many of the boys drowned immediately.

PART 1 | UNDERSTANDING SUFFERING

Mo saw that happen to some of his friends. Other boys swam but were killed by shards of broken wood hurtling through the death wave like spears. Mo saw them die too. He clung to a tree and looked down at the dirty brown waves carrying bodies, animals, cars, debris and boats up to five kilometres inland.

The wave finally flowed back to sea. When the water receded, Mo returned home. He found that his house and everything around it had been smashed to pieces. No one in his family had survived. Not one person. So he had no home to sleep in, no parents to hug and feed him, no sister to console him. No one.

What did Mo do to deserve such suffering?

Everyone's heart goes out to a child who suffers, whether they know them personally or see them on the news media. Mine always does. Sometimes it makes me weep as I watch the news.

Some of the local religious leaders in Aceh thought they knew the reason for the tsunami. They said it was a manifestation of the wrath of God: the town had allowed too many tourists who drank alcohol and dressed far too inappropriately for a Muslim province under Sharia law. Some Hindus describes it as 'karma', a balancing of the books for previous sins. These were similar to explanations commonly found among Christians—the notion that suffering is a manifestation of God's anger or disappointment with them because of sin: 'My child was born disabled because I had an affair with my secretary at an office Christmas party five years ago.'

This is a misconception, as we will see in a moment. But if this explanation is not true, then why *does* God allow such things as natural disasters and pandemics? How can the loving God I trust actually permit this—and not only permit it but make it clear that such things are inevitable? And that he will not stop them happening?

> *There will be great earthquakes, famines and pestilences in various places.*
> Luke 21:11

'When we suffer it is logical to ask, 'Why the heck am I down here in this valley of suffering?' This is the starting point for exploring the Christian view of suffering. It is in thinking about the 'why' question that we can begin to cope with our own suffering or the suffering of those we care for, and begin to develop greater resilience.

Barriers to understanding

Three misconceptions make understanding suffering harder for Christians than it should be. These misconceptions are major barriers to moving forward, and it can be difficult to get through them. They are:

Misconception 1: Suffering is *punishment*.

Misconception 2: Suffering *should be avoidable*.

Misconception 3: Suffering should be *explainable*.

If these misconceptions are ignored, swept under the carpet, over-theologized, over-philosophized or trivialized in the church, it can lead to anguish. It can also challenge the faith of believers who are on a journey of personal suffering, struggling in their own faith with the issue or unable to give clear answers about it to their children or friends. Believers can expend a lot of emotional energy on thoughts like these:

- I must have done something to deserve this.' (And knowing what that is will be my escape from the suffering.)
- 'God could and should have provided a detour around this valley of suffering.' (God needs to remove all suffering—he's made a cruel mistake.)
- 'I must get an answer to why my suffering exists.' (And if I don't, I can't believe in a God who would allow such suffering and then not explain himself clearly.)

We need to consider biblical responses to these three misconceptions. I call these responses the three INs of suffering: Innocence, Inevitability and Incomprehensibility.

Misconception 1: Suffering is punishment

The first misconception is that suffering happens to us because we deserve it. 'Her cancer was a punishment for her bitter anger towards her mother.' 'The earthquake happened because that town turned its back on God.' 'If you have sex before big exams God will make you fail.' Have you ever felt that sort of 'I must deserve this' feeling?

Deep in human nature there is a desire to find a correlation between bad behaviour and bad circumstances (and between good behaviour and blessings). Human sacrifice to appease vengeful deities was practised in ancient Mesoamerican and Peruvian societies, and animal sacrifice was part of many cultures including the Greek, Hebrew, Roman and Egyptian. This shows how culture influences the way we think about suffering. Today it is no different. We hear stories of suffering on the media, in movies and around the water cooler, and deep down we think that things might be deserved and undeserved.

> **DEEP DOWN IN HUMAN NATURE IS A DESIRE TO FIND A CORRELATION BETWEEN BAD BEHAVIOR AND BAD CIRCUMSTANCES**

We see this when some Christians look in natural disasters and epidemics for messages from God in terms of judgment. Commenting on the HIV epidemic, the evangelist Billy Graham asked an audience 'Is AIDS a judgment of God?' and answered his own question: 'I could not say for sure, but I think so.' Although he later apologised for suggesting that God may have let this terrible disease loose on homosexuals, promiscuous heterosexuals and IV drug users to judge them, his comment evoked a lot of social commentary on the link between actions and suffering. The notion of AIDS as God's judgment was hard for most people to accept, including those who developed HIV after blood transfusions.

Any notion that God's frustration with society would lead to an epidemic misunderstands what Jesus said early in his ministry about judgmentalism and sends community views of Christianity back to the Dark Ages. Moreover, seeing natural disasters as 'acts of God'—as if God deliberately punished people by sending calamities—is completely wrong. In fact, God created the universe and the laws of nature, and natural disasters are the result of those laws working themselves out. If God is to be blamed for disasters, he should also be given credit for the wonderful way that nature nurtures, feeds and warms us, and for how few disasters actually occur. As someone who has studied the human body in detail, I am less amazed that diseases happen than that they do not!

> ANY NOTION THAT GOD'S FRUSTRATION
> WITH SOCIETY WOULD LEAD TO AN EPIDEMIC
> MISUNDERSTANDS WHAT JESUS SAID

Humans have high levels of 'suggestibility'. 'Suggestibility' is the basis of superstitions like Friday the 13th and touching wood for good luck. We inherit that tendency in our DNA—it goes with being human, like walking upright. Because of that, it is easy to get hooked into the notion that our suffering is due to something that displeases God. One example is when a past family member has 'toyed with evil' and someone says, 'My grandfather participated in occult games such as Ouija boards and séances, and that's why I am suffering now.'

But do you really think that God would look at you, weeping as he does for you, and make that happen? God certainly hates evil (1 Cor. 6:9–10), and decisions that parents and grandparents make can affect innocent children so that they suffer the natural consequences of those choices. However, superstitious thinking about personal and inter-generational suffering is just another way that we search for guilt as an explanation of suffering instead of living in the freedom and grace God offers us.

> *I did sometimes think that I had a disabled son because I had done something wrong. That was more a physical thing, such as maybe I used too much bleach in the bathroom or did something else, rather than it being a spiritual thing about sin. Ironically, it was people who are non-Christians that said things like 'What did you do in another life for this to happen?' Sometimes a thought would creep in that maybe we were being punished because we had been enjoying life too much and we were being called to order, like Job. But then I realized that wasn't true—we are encouraged to enjoy life to the full.*
> *Judith Curtis, personal interview*

The innocent suffer

Against the idea that suffering is punishment, the Bible makes it clear that innocent people suffer. Indeed, many of the psalms cry out to God about this:

> *Surely in vain I have kept my heart pure and have washed my hands in innocence. All day long I have been afflicted, and every morning brings new punishments.*
> *Psalm 73:13–14*

It is not a question of *deserving* suffering. When standing at the grave of a young mother killed by a drunk driver, it does not help to say that such suffering is anything other than deeply sad. It just happened. No matter how often atheists present awful examples of human suffering, as a Christian I can only agree with them. Such suffering is desperately tragic. But if you are looking for answers to the suffering of individuals, don't look for God's angry vengeance at the guilt of the innocent—it won't be there. While you weep beside the young mother's coffin, God is weeping too.

The innocent will suffer

Dropping the 'guilt' accusation on sufferers, even subtly, is deeply hurtful: 'You must have done something that God doesn't like' or 'You must *not* have done something God thinks is important' (for example, not prayed enough). No, no, no! Please don't do that to people who are suffering. It only makes their pain so much worse. And it's just plain wrong.

This desire to link sin to suffering created two situations that allowed Jesus to deal clearly with it. One involved a blind man.

> *As he went along, he saw a man blind from birth. His disciples*
> *asked him, 'Rabbi, who sinned, this man or his parents, that*
> *he was born blind?'*
> *'Neither this man nor his parents sinned,' said Jesus, 'but this*
> *happened so that the works of God might be displayed in him'.*
> *John 9:1–2*

Because the disciples made the error of thinking that only 'guilty' people suffer, they assumed personal guilt in the blind man or his parents. Jesus corrected them. The man's blindness was not the result of any personal sin, not a result of karma. Instead, Jesus said, 'This happened so that the works of God might be displayed in him.' This is an example of one way Jesus wants us to consider suffering—not to keep looking back and asking 'why', but to look forward and ask, 'What outcome might this suffering have?'

On another occasion, recorded in Luke 13, Jesus referred to some people who had been killed in an accident. He asked, 'Those eighteen who died when the tower in Siloam fell on them—do you think they were more guilty than all the others living in Jerusalem?' Again he replied clearly, 'I tell you, no! But unless you repent, you too will all perish.' What was going through Jesus' mind when he mentioned that accident? God's revenge? Faulty construction practices? God's plan? Or the lesson to be learnt? Again he was asking people not to think retrospectively about why this happened but prospectively about what outcome might occur if they didn't learn from the event.

In these two stories Jesus made it clear that suffering is not the product of personal sin. He certainly reminded us that we live in a world of sin that has consequences, so we should each examine this and change our ways. But he never blamed the victims. He never said to those who were suffering, 'Suck it up, you're getting your just deserts' (and he never said 'you should show more faith by accepting it' or 'you haven't prayed enough). Instead he was moved with compassion for them, healing many. He definitely did not use his enormous power to punish people.

If you want to grasp the notion of innocents suffering, re-read the Psalms. And if you want to soak up the idea that we are called to respond in compassion like Jesus did, not to pass judgment, re-read the parable of the Good Samaritan. The Samaritan could have looked at the man who was mugged and thought, 'This is just the will of God. He must have sinned.' But he didn't. He stopped and helped, at great cost and risk to himself.

To me, the most convincing summary of suffering and innocence from Christian scholars is that we are innocent but can learn from tragedies. They can draw us closer to God or cause us to pull back from him. Suffering is part of this general message, but it can't be reverse-engineered to say that any particular event was caused by God as a message or punishment. A casual reading of Romans 8:28 can make people think that all suffering is good. It is not good, but it can be worked on by God, in partnership with us and our response to it, to make it into something good.

Some suffering, of course, *is* self-inflicted, the natural consequence of our actions—for example, getting drunk, driving into a tree and becoming a paraplegic or taking drugs and becoming an addict. Sometimes Christians who don't think through this issue equate the notion of ' bearing the cross' (1 Peter 4:15) with problems resulting directly from sins of commission or omission. This over-spiritualizes their suffering and thus perpetuates it.

But suffering also happens to innocent people, believers and non-believers alike. It just does. Often. Looking backwards all the time won't provide much help, but looking forward will.

If it is you who is innocently suffering, I encourage you in love to stop always lifting up stones and looking underneath for an answer to the question, 'What did I do to deserve this?' Don't waste your time and sweat imagining why God is punishing you. You won't find answers that way.

Misconception 2: Suffering should be avoidable

I have been asked hundreds of times in my life why God allows tragedy and suffering. I have to confess that I really do not know the answer totally, even to my own satisfaction. I have to accept, by faith, that God is sovereign, and He is a God of love and mercy and compassion in the midst of suffering.
Billy Graham[3]

The second misconception is that suffering should be avoidable in life. Small sufferings are OK, but not the really painful stuff. Surely they're not part of God's plan. Wouldn't he prefer to remove all suffering in life and heal everybody who has enough faith? God should provide detours around suffering, and if he doesn't, we wonder why.

It is easy to feel ambushed and bewildered when suffering happens. Life is going along, busy and hard yet full of joy... and then we fall into a valley of suffering. We don't choose to do so and there is no warning. 'I found a lump in my breast that turned out to be terminal cancer.' 'My baby girl got hit by a car while riding her tricycle.' Then life turns black and there is no escape. I am in this valley of pain, and I want to know why it couldn't have been avoided.

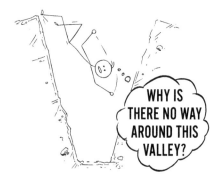

.Couldn't God have provided a detour?

When I was young, I felt as if I was made of steel. I had only experienced minor physical sufferings (such as football injuries) and the kind of distant suffering that moves one's heart at the time (such as the assassination of President Kennedy). I assumed people could just snap out of any problems they had and toughen up.

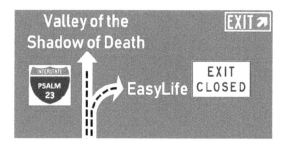

No detour available

When I became a Christian, I began to see much more profound suffering, especially as a medical student. I also started to notice that the Bible says suffering is inevitable. Then I heard preachers say from the pulpit that suffering is inevitable. That started to wake me up. I read Psalm 23 and realised there is no detour around 'the valley of the shadow of death'—the valley of suffering. Christians are not exempt from cancer, tsunamis, terrorism, martyrdom, depression or any other form of suffering. The Bible clearly describes the suffering of God's most faithful servants, including torture, stoning and being sawed in half.

All of that made me a bit nervous. I was never going to avoid major suffering. Please, God, not me. The inevitability of suffering sounded awful and heartless.

Biblical statements about the inevitability of suffering are not just isolated verses but occur all the way from Genesis to Revelation. Amazingly, there is no airbrushing of the inevitability of suffering from the Bible. It is not a 'dirty little secret' kept hidden from readers or edited out. This would have been curious if the writers had simply been trying to sell an attractive product. But they were not. They were explaining to us the nature of God and how he views life, including suffering. Suffering is not only unavoidable; it is explicitly guaranteed to happen.

> *My heart is in anguish within me; the terrors of death have fallen on me. Fear and trembling have beset me; horror has overwhelmed me.*
> *Psalm 55:4–5*

> *Nation will rise against nation, and kingdom against kingdom. There will be famines and earthquakes in various places.*
> *Matthew 24:7*

> *You may have had to suffer grief in all kinds of trials.*
> *1 Peter 1:67*

Of course, some Christians believe that although suffering happens, God does not really *want* it to happen. This is especially so with sickness —they think that healing is available for every Christian if they just have sufficient faith. I hear that often in the context of faith healing for my patients. It can be difficult to navigate. There is an important difference between healing that *may* happen and healing that *will* happen. I am sure that miraculous healing (or amazing responses to medical treatment after prayer) occurs for Christians. But it is not common, including in those with massive faith. We have all seen that.

What is more common is that we are required to understand our suffering, and the suffering of those we care about, from the point of view of its inevitability, and then to respond appropriately. The Bible shows us the inevitability of suffering, not just as a partial explanation for it, but as a foundation for acceptance so that we can be ready to face it.

The inevitability of suffering is hard to take. It makes me try to understand why God would want it this way. The reason is clear: we don't grow much without it. That is the common experience. As hard as it is, how we respond to inevitable suffering determines if we do or don't grow, if we are paralysed by fear or able to look ahead. I encourage you to accept this inevitability.

Misconception 3: Suffering should be explainable

The third misconception is that the Bible gives a crystal-clear explanation of suffering, and that all we have to do is study it thoroughly and pray and we will understand what that explanation is. We will then have all the answers we need—for ourselves, for those who are suffering, for their loved ones and for any atheist who challenges us on the subject.

I am sorry to report that this is impossible. The more thoroughly one reads the Bible, the more it becomes clear we will never understand suffering completely.

This is the third IN of suffering: Incomprehensibility. More precisely, suffering is not so much incomprehensible as *incompletely comprehensible*. Mystery is not a lack of information and understanding—it is incomplete understanding.

This is expressed in the Old Testament, including through the trials of Job. There it is made clear that human knowledge of how and why things happen is limited. If we achieve massive data knowledge of the world, complete with artificial intelligence to predict and even determine outcomes, along with a detailed understanding of physics and the universe, we will still only ever glimpse God. We will still only see a tiny fraction of reality.

> *Where were you when I laid the earth's foundation? Tell me,*
> *if you have understanding... Have you comprehended the*
> *vast expanse of the earth? Tell me, if you know all this.*
> *Job 38:4, 18*

Similarly, in the New Testament Paul makes it clear that our understanding of things is like looking into an imperfect mirror that doesn't reflect images well. We will only see clearly later when we meet God.

> **SUFFERING IS NOT INCOMPREHENSIBLE BUT INCOMPLETELY COMPREHENSIBLE**

Now we see things imperfectly, like puzzling reflections in a mirror, but then we will see everything with perfect clarity.
1 Corinthians 13:12 (NLT)

MY PERSONAL SEARCH FOR ANSWERS

I think I came out of my mother's womb as a scientist, always wanting answers to 'why?' All young children ask 'why?' incessantly, but I never stopped. This is what has driven a lot of my career in medicine. It is also what led me into faith from an unchurched family (I kept asking, 'Who designed this brilliant thing called the human body?'); drove me out of it ('Why are there no answers to the key questions like suffering?'); then drew me back into it again ('Christianity is rational after all').

The modern scientific world is obsessed with understanding, and so am I as a professional scientist. But it is not always possible to get it, and to me this is terribly frustrating.

For many years I have searched for clear answers to questions of faith, and I have found many. To try to understand the issue of suffering I have lifted up as many stones as I could, looking for nuggets of gold beneath them to throw light on why God allows it. Finally, after years of seeing suffering up close and reading about it in the works of leading Christian scholars, I realised that there *is* no clear answer. We will certainly not get a clear view of our suffering while we are going through it, and, although it may become clear afterwards, it may *never* become clear in this life, only in the next.

> *Trust in the* LORD *with all your heart, and lean not on your own understanding. In all your ways acknowledge Him him [His will and purpose for your life], and He shall direct your paths.*
> *Proverbs 3:5–6* (NKJV)

It can be hard to accept the fact that we see this issue reflected in a misty mirror, through a window blurred by raindrops. We can glimpse some things, but the whole picture is never going to be clear.

Yet we have many examples in life where we can only glimpse part of the whole—things we can only understand after the event is fully seen and which create mystery until then. I am sure you have worked with jigsaw puzzles. Imagine undertaking a puzzle without the picture on the box. You would begin by finding similar pieces and gradually build up bits that make sense. It would not be until you finished or were shown the picture on the box that you would get the full understanding of each piece.

It is similar with digital images. If you zoom into any part of a digital image, you will see just a few coloured pixels. Zoom out a bit and you will start to make more sense of it. Look at the whole image and you will see it fully. The same is true with modern movies that use CGI to put actors into scenes that only exist in a computer. It's not until you see the finished picture that you understand the full reality that the director knew all along.

When I was a child there was an artist on children's TV who painted weird pictures on four panels, lines and curves that made no sense. At the end she would rotate each of the panels and everything would become clear. That is what it will be like for us as we live longer and/or when we meet God. Plenty of people have seen answers to their personal suffering in their lifetime, but only on later reflection. They have looked back and seen how the suffering has changed their lives (this is certainly true for me). However, in many cases we will never understand our suffering in this life. Job never found out what happened to cause his suffering; his questions were never answered. He was helpless at that point and just had to accept it. For us, too, understanding may have to wait for the next life—but we will know sometime.

I didn't continually ask why? why? why? I know there's never an answer to that question, and I knew that fact before Paul got terminal cancer and before we had a disabled child. I learned it years ago when I read Edith Schaeffer's book on suffering. In it she says there will be suffering, it's inevitable, and you won't get an answer to the 'why?' question.

We're never going to understand why suffering happens and why it is inevitable. But we know that God has used us and our experience of suffering to help others. Also, having a disabled child has helped our other three children become more compassionate and kind. It has shaped them, and they acknowledge that.

Judith Curtis

I am still silently crying out to God for a sign that Ciara is all right but at the same time questioning the very existence of this God who let me down so completely, in such a devastating way. If God is omnipotent, why didn't he keep Ciara safe? If he is all caring, how can he stand by and watch humanity suffer so much?

Gradually I come to the realisation that my quest is futile, that life and death are mysteries that humankind has not fathomed, that no amount of reading will provide me with answers. The knowledge that I am seeking will have to emerge from within; it will have to be a felt knowledge, an experienced knowledge, not gleaned by way of the intellect.

Una Glennon, mother of murdered daughter[4]

Personally I have accepted that in this life I will only see how a portion of the jigsaw puzzle pieces fit together, and that I will only know the full picture at the end. I have accepted that I probably won't get a clear answer quickly, and possibly never in this lifetime. It was the same for Job and Paul. I hope that you too can find this acceptance of incomprehensibility.

Mystery underlies all Christian views on suffering

The three INs—Innocence, Inevitability and Incomprehensibility—cause us to view suffering as a mystery. I know that mystery is not usually a satisfactory answer for those who are grieving, angry, frustrated and deeply wounded. We want to know why; we want solutions. I respect those who have these feelings, and I empathise with them in their pain.

When Christians have been on the journey for some time, they often find it easier to accept the mystery of their faith. I like Phillip Yancey's analogy: we are like fish in a home aquarium, and God is like the aquarium owner who comes by as a shadow, providing a healthy environment and food for the fish and seeming to enjoy them, yet mostly incomprehensible to them. Because of Jesus we understand a lot more about God than that, yet in the end he remains only partly comprehensible.

I should mention that although mystery underlies all Christian views on suffering, there are several ways that theologians look at it. Simplistically put, one is the 'Blueprint model', which sees God as having a specific plan for every aspect of our lives, from the person we marry to the job we do, and our suffering fits into that plan. Another approach is the 'Warfare model', which sees suffering primarily as the result of the battle between God and Satan. Mystery is a component of these views too. But I think that seeing mystery primarily as a way of engaging existentially with suffering is a biblical way to approach it. And it is a strong platform for faith, not a weak one.

Understanding the mystery of suffering includes the deep realization that God does not sit in the stands with his arms folded, watching dispassionately as the suffering happens down in the arena. He is not indifferent to suffering like a stern, unsympathetic father or a Roman emperor watching gladiators in the Colosseum. Rather, unlike other 'gods', he has entered into that suffering, most manifestly in Jesus coming to the earth. This 'entering in' has helped me to understand more about God's view of suffering. At a minimum I now realise that he does not seek to eradicate suffering but enters into it with us. (This is discussed in more detail in the next chapter.)

God is not a stern, indifferent father

What I have learnt about the Christian view of suffering, then, is both weird and wonderful. It is weird because not only does God not stop natural disasters and human evil, he chooses not to make it clear why this is so. But it is also wonderful because he enters into that suffering himself, even at the highest imaginable level. He doesn't stand back aloof and uncaring. It breaks his heart (quite reasonably, I think) and he weeps. He promises that he is able to partner with us to turn suffering into something that makes us better people and helps us to better serve others.

> *The wise man in the storm prays to God, not for safety from danger, but for deliverance from fear.*
> *Ralph Waldo Emerson*[5]

Anger with God

Because Christianity refuses to provide a precise and ultimately crystal -clear explanation for suffering, it is easy to feel frustrated and angry. When that happens, some Christians feel like they are showing a lack of faith. Yet one thing that is clear from the Bible is that such an expression of anger is not sinful. Indeed, God encourages and welcomes it. As John Dickson says:

> *Psalm 23 is well known. But the psalm immediately before it opens with a cry of doubt that you'd expect from a skeptic rather than a believer. Both may have had the same composer.*

> *My God, my God, we have you forsaken me?*
>   *Why are you so far from saving me,*
>   *so far from the words of my groaning?*
> *Oh my God, I cry out by day, but you do not answer,*
>   *by night, and am not silent.*

> *Such a cry to a Buddhist would indicate un-enlightenment, to a Muslim, faithlessness, bordering on blasphemy, and for an atheist, meaninglessness.*

> *The God of the Bible bids us to approach him with our doubts, our fears, and our frustrations. It is in this mode of personal engagement, shouting at God, that God whispers back his rather unexpected replies.*
> *John Dickson[6]*

Many of the psalms shout at God, pleading for a better future in the midst of suffering. They are not written to describe a heartless God but to encourage us to take our anger and frustration to a loving Father. A similarly positive view of anger is expressed by theologian Henri Nouwen, who sees the spiritual benefit of anger directed towards God written in both the Old and New Testaments.

> **IT IS OK TO PLEAD FOR A BETTER FUTURE**
> **AND TO EXPRESS ANGER TOWARDS GOD**

It is clear that only by expressing our anger and hatred directly to God will we come to know the fullness of both his love and our freedom.
Henri Noewen[7]

Perhaps could it be that knowing all things for certain would prevent us from experiencing the full life of faith?

Would it really help us to know exactly why God permits a specific instance of suffering? Such awareness may engender even more bitterness. But it does help our actual condition when we turn to him in trust. It can break down self-sufficiency and create in us a profound new level of faith in God. It can transform our suffering into qualities of lasting, even eternal, value.
Phillip Yancey[8]

Beyond the misconceptions

I have found that, once considered and understood, the three INs of suffering can be put aside and only looked at every now and again. I imagine them placed in a bedside drawer—not needing to be taken out every day but just now and then, to be reminded. If embraced they can become part of your life, an almost automatic frame of reference that helps you to move on.

I have further found that a key to managing suffering is to stop looking backwards every day and asking 'why?' Once you know that you are innocent, that suffering is inevitable and that explanations will always be partial, you are in a position to look forward and know how to respond.

Of course, ultimately that may all be unsatisfying for some. But as God said to Job, 'You don't know how to make or run a universe, but I do. So please trust me and leave it up to me.'

The murder of our daughter is a tragedy so public that there is no escape in Perth. Many times in banks, shops and other public places, total strangers just pour out their sorrows. This enables me to see that we are not alone. That many, many people are carrying similar, some heavier, burdens.
It further confirms my belief that we live in a suffering world. Somehow, for some inexplicable reason, suffering is an integral part of the human condition. We cannot escape it.
As I open the New Testament at a familiar passage, the words suddenly appear to come towards me like the zoom through a telephoto lens. They appear larger and clearer and brighter. It is as if I am reading them for the first time, at a different level of understanding. I continue to read, unable

to put down the book. Jesus showed us in no uncertain way by his crucifixion and death that this is the suffering world; that we will all suffer, that suffering is somehow embedded in the very blueprint of humanity. The absurdity of the crucifixion does have meaning after all.
Una Glennon[9]

You can choose to remain frustrated and angry, and that might be totally reasonable and understandable for some time. However, in the next chapter I will discuss four powerful promises that provide daily reminders of God's promises for those who are suffering. Those promises are a ladder you can use to climb out of the valley of suffering whenever you fall into it. I encourage you in love to consider them.

Key points

- Suffering is not punishment. Searching for something you have done to deserve it is fruitless.
- Suffering is not avoidable. There is no detour around the valley of suffering.
- Suffering is not explainable. Don't expect a crystal-clear answer to this question.
- Mystery underlies all Christian views on suffering.
- God suffers and weeps alongside us.
- It is not sinful to get angry with God when you don't understand.

NON-CHRISTIAN VIEWS OF WHY SUFFERING HAPPENS

Alongside the Christian view, I want to briefly note some non-Christian views of suffering to provide a fuller understanding of the spectrum of approaches that humans have taken to try to make sense of it. Suffering is important in most religions, including explanations of its existence (more important in some religions than others) and how to respond to it. This issue is also important to atheists.

Hinduism: suffering is karma (payback)

Hinduism. Hinduism is the world's oldest religion and the third largest religion behind Christianity and Islam. Almost all of its followers are in India. Hinduism teaches that all suffering, including the sorts of suffering experienced in India such as famine, disease, floods and poverty, are due to *karma*. This is a universal principle whereby all actions of the past are balanced out by present events. Suffering follows naturally from negative behaviours in this life or in a previous life. Suffering is to be accepted as the just consequence of such actions. It is also an opportunity for spiritual progress. It is payback, it is deserved and it is fate.

Buddhism: suffering is caused by desire

Buddhism. Buddhism was born out of an environment of suffering. It does not attempt to reconcile evil with God as monotheistic religions do but considers suffering and evil to be illusions. It is because you desire too much that you suffer—you love your child and she dies, so it was your love that caused your suffering. Stop desiring the love so much. Suffering from illness is because of your desire to be healthy. We must train ourselves to see through these illusions. Get free of this and suffering disappears.

Islam: suffering is the will of Allah

Islam. Islam follows the teachings laid out in the Koran plus the teachings and example of Muhammad written in the Hadith. It has nearly two billion followers. Islam sees suffering and evil events as ultimately the will of Allah, so one needs to submit to it all. This is not the automatic biochemical determinism of scientists but the personal will of God. The powerful, all-knowing and benevolent God creates everything, including human suffering and evil. The faithful must endure suffering and not question why—it is a test of faith and even a blessing.

Atheism. Atheism holds that there is no God, just a random closed system of events governed by the physics of the universe. Things such as earthquakes, tsunamis and volcanoes are just the automatic outworking of those laws of nature. None of these events are morally good or bad. If anyone suffers, there is no point in looking for answers or comfort—the universe is indifferent.

> *In a universe of blind physical forces and genetic replication, some people are going to get hurt, other people are going to get lucky, and you won't find any rhyme or reason in it, nor any justice.*
> **Richard Dawkins**[10]

Since God doesn't exist, atheists hold that there is no point in complaining to him about suffering. Yet they also argue that suffering is precisely what calls the existence of God into question. As Bertrand Russell said, 'No one can believe in a good God if they've sat at the bedside of a dying child.' Evil means that any God that does exist must be intrinsically heartless or immoral.

I always have to think too of a little boy sitting on the banks of a river in West Africa who has a worm boring through his eyeball, turning him blind before he's five years old. And I reply and say, 'Well, presumably the God you speak about created the worm as well,' and now, I find it baffling to credit a merciful God with that action.
Sir David Attenborough[11]

The suffering of innocent children is a crushing, intolerable burden, and to many this makes the Christian promise of a future heaven a heartless response to such suffering. They reasonably want release from this suffering *now*. And so do Christians. Yet though I can fully empathise with the atheist's distress in the face of suffering, I have noticed that the comments of angry atheists are often based on ignorance of the *actual* Christian view of suffering.

THE COMMENTS OF ANGRY ATHEISTS ARE OFTEN BASED ON IGNORANCE OF THE CHRISTIAN VIEW OF SUFFERING

In summary:

- Hinduism invites you to accept evil as your *karma*.
- Buddhism invites you extinguish your desires and become enlightened.
- Islam invites you to accept things as the will of God.
- Atheism invites you to accept that evil is part of an indifferent universe.

PART 2

Surviving Suffering

CHAPTER 3

Enduring and growing from suffering

My wife developed a lump in her breast. I was really scared as each test was undertaken. Then the biopsy same back as cancer. Hearing that news made me burst into tears, and every day for the next few weeks I would find myself sobbing alone in my study or in the car.
The Author

> The purpose of this chapter is to discuss spiritual and practical aspects of coping with suffering. It explores four key promises God has given us and introduces the 'Diamond Prayer' as a helpful way of using Jesus' example to stop, pray and focus on these promises when it is otherwise hard to do.

Sometimes you are so down that it feels like another hit will destroy you. At such times it can be hard to feel like anyone really understands or cares. You know that the Bible says you will grow from suffering but it doesn't seem to be happening. And that makes you feel worse.

How can a Christian move through suffering and grow from it? Some people do it well—but how? What does the Bible say?

God has given us four key promises that are helpful in navigating the valley of suffering. They enable a sufferer not only to survive the valley but to glimpse the possibility of growing and blooming. They are not four self-help steps but biblical promises to remember, meditate on, embrace and prayerfully ponder daily.

We need to take God's hand as we push through any time of suffering. He will be there for us, but he does expect us to be partners in the process. We can knock his hand away or take it, decline his help or accept it.

> *Consider him who endured such opposition from sinners, so that you will not grow weary and lose heart.*
> *Hebrews 12:3*

> *Therefore we do not lose heart. Though outwardly we are wasting away, yet inwardly we are being renewed day by day.*
> *2 Corinthians 4:16*

As we come to consider this, I want to acknowledge again the anguish that many feel when they are in the valley of suffering. Under such circumstances it can be difficult to think about these promises—the suffering is too overwhelming. And it is not possible at that point to contemplate climbing out of the valley—sufferers can be disillusioned, angry, exhausted and barely able to function. They can feel forsaken. It can take time.

But God does walk with us. Sometimes we will feel it and sometimes not, but the same psalm of David that describes the valley of suffering also provides encouragement.

> *Even though I walk through the valley of the shadow of death, I will fear no evil, for you are with me; your rod and your staff, they comfort me.*
> *Psalm 23:4*

How suffering crept up on me

Jacqui and I during her breast cancer therapy

I thought I knew a lot about handling suffering, but I have learnt more about it in the last few years—at the personal level, the Psalm 23 heart level—than at any time in my life. Let me tell you why.

I've had a tough few years. I don't mind admitting this. Actually, I do mind admitting it—I am honestly not good at admitting such hardships. I don't know whether it's because I'm a male or just shy and reluctant to share. But the last few years have changed this. What happened?

First, my wife Jacqui developed a lump in her breast. Hearing that news made me burst into tears, and every day for the next few weeks I would find myself sobbing alone in my study or in the car. I was really scared as each test was undertaken and the results examined. When the biopsy came back as breast cancer with lymph node involvement, I wept. Then followed operations, chemotherapy and radiation, all of which knocked her around, and me along with it. I had to confront the reality that the love of my life might die. I still get teary talking about it. Many reading this will know that feeling well.

As if that wasn't enough, during Jacqui's chemotherapy I developed a problem in my right eye, a curious, unexplainable form of unilateral glaucoma. The problem seemed less important in the scheme of things than Jacqui's cancer, so I didn't mention it much, but it was progressing and threatening to make me blind in that eye.

In addition, during this time I faced challenges in my workplace leadership roles, mostly to do with managing strong personality clashes around academic issues. I was required to try to facilitate resolution but got emotionally wounded myself in the crossfire. I tend to ruminate on such things at night and am easily disillusioned by people behaving in ungracious, critical ways. It got so bad that at several points I considered resigning. This was made even worse by the fact that I also suffer from SAD (seasonal affective disorder), a condition whereby one's mood declines during winter. It is a biological problem linked to the amount of light hitting the retina. It is easily treated by getting lots of sunshine into the eye, and I normally do that. But I neglected this, and whenever I awoke and found the day was overcast, I immediately felt disappointed and low.

'Winter blues'

Finally, while working as a doctor after the 2018 Indonesian earthquake and tsunami in Sulawesi, I became utterly exhausted. I had little sleep at night and worked extremely hard during the day, all in difficult, hot, frustrating conditions and entirely in a foreign language. To cap it all, I developed septicaemia, which required intravenous antibiotics. For several weeks I could not eat and was barely able get out of bed.

I am telling you this because I have to admit that it all got to me, sneaking up on me when I wasn't paying attention. It made me suffer every day. And although some of that suffering was physical, mostly it was emotional. I neglected self-care.

All of this was happening in the same period. This was tough, but it had one advantage: it made me think much more existentially about personal suffering and how to cope with it. And it made me a lot more open to talking to my wife and friends about my challenges rather than just asking them about theirs.

The four promises

During the difficult times described above, the example of Jesus became a model for me. Jesus sometimes retreated to be in communion with God when he was peopled-out. I imagine he may have been remembering and thinking about his Father's promises to him before praying specifically for what was on his heart.

I decided to do the same. I discovered that this quiet communion was a deeper way of communing with God, and it was magnificently helpful to me. I developed what I call the 'Diamond Prayer'—a prayer meditation based on four key promises from the Bible that gave me great comfort in my suffering. It helped me take hold of those promises and draw strength from them.

Here are the four promises that God has given us to help us survive and grow from suffering:

- Promise 1: You are indestructible. He will not let the essential 'you' be destroyed.
- Promise 2: God understands your suffering, even if no one else does. He's been there.
- Promise 3: Jesus loves you deeply. He is filled with compassion for you, weeps for you and does so unconditionally.
- Promise 4: You will grow and bloom like a flower because of this suffering. You will be transformed into a better version of yourself, and that transformation will help others to bloom as well as you pass it on.

I will first discuss each of these promises in turn and then explain the Diamond Prayer.

PROMISE 1:
YOU ARE INDESTRUCTIBLE

Sometimes we feel like we will be destroyed by our suffering—'It is all too much for me. I am drowning.' I have felt that, and maybe you have too. Yet God promises us that this will not happen. The essential 'us' cannot be destroyed. And although physical bodies will end (we all get old, we get sick, we die), God promises to watch over us in this life and provide a high level of care and preservation, keeping us from being crushed by our suffering.

> *We are hard pressed on every side, but not crushed; perplexed, but not in despair; persecuted, but not abandoned; struck down, but not destroyed.*
> *2 Corinthians 4:8–9*

THE ESSENTIAL 'YOU' IS VALUABLE TO GOD AND CANNOT BE DESTROYED IN THIS LIFE OR THE NEXT

As Christians we know there is an essential 'you'. Being human we are all made in the image of God, so we share some commonness, but each of us is also a one-of-a-kind, limited edition. We are known before we are born (Jer 1:5; Gal 1:15; Eph 1:3–4) and will continue on after we die. There are different theological ways of thinking about that and different words used ('soul', 'spirit'), but they all lead to the unique and indestructible 'you'.

That 'you' is special to God. He numbers every hair on your head (Matt 10:30) and loves you deeply. Although the body around it can be challenged, the essential 'you' cannot be destroyed. Some people, like me, find this promise very encouraging.

When I think about our indestructibility, I think of a large diamond in a house. I imagine that house totally collapsing during an earthquake then being further smashed by an ensuing tsunami. The building is ruined, but the diamond survives, indestructible.

In a world where suffering is inevitable, this fact provides hope at times when it is hard to find any. Although we are not promised ultimate *physical* indestructibility, we are assured by God that the essential 'you' is indestructible in both this life and the next.

> *For I am convinced that neither death nor life, neither angels nor demons, neither the present nor the future, nor any powers, neither height nor depth, nor anything else in all creation, will be able to separate us from the love of God that is in Christ Jesus our Lord.*
> *Romans 8:38–39*

Of course, while verses like these mean that we can reasonably expect protection in this life, that is not always the case. If I am in a plane and a wing falls off, I know my time is up. At that point my faith in my indestructibility is for the next life (Twink Parry was in that position when her bus crashed in Thailand). This is particularly important for those whose chronic suffering will only be relieved by having a new body.

> *The creation itself will be liberated from its bondage to decay and brought into the freedom and glory of the children of God.*
> *Romans 8:21*

Listen, I tell you a mystery: We will not all sleep, but we will all be changed—in a flash, in the twinkling of an eye, at the last trumpet. For the trumpet will sound, the dead will be raised imperishable, and we will be changed.
1 Corinthians 15:51–52

Myth: My suffering is just too great—it will crush me and God can't save me from it. It will break me.

Meditation: I am a diamond. I can be beaten, heated and put under all sorts of pressure, but nothing can ultimately crush or destroy the essential me.

PROMISE 2:
HE UNDERSTANDS BECAUSE HE'S BEEN THERE

We all like to be understood and hate to be misunderstood. It is awful during a period of suffering if no one recognises what you are going through. It becomes even worse if your friends or family trivialise what you have experienced.

This is not just a null feeling; it is a hurtful feeling. I have looked after many war veterans in my medical practice and most are reluctant to talk about their war experiences. This is a common experience of others also. One of the reasons for this is that they are afraid the listener won't understand and will say something inappropriate. Given that no one except another person who has been through the same thing can really comprehend it, they shield themselves.

The same applies to first responders such as police, paramedics and firefighters.

When I returned from my first trip to Aceh as a volunteer after the 2004 Indian Ocean tsunami, I was an emotional wreck. The morning after I got home, my pastor asked if I would be willing to be interviewed at church about my work there, but I told him I couldn't possibly get through it. I would just break down and cry. The next day I went to work at my hospital, still feeling like I could cry at any moment, and the first secretary I saw (a lovely lady) asked me, 'Did you have a good time in Aceh?' I didn't blame her—she didn't understand—but it surprised me how inappropriate and hurtful the question felt. Nobody else asked me any appropriate questions either, but I didn't hold it against them (I remember asking a medical colleague similarly inappropriate questions myself when he returned from working as a doctor in Rwanda after the massacres there). I longed for someone who had worked in disaster situations to talk to, but there was no one, so I carried it around myself.

Have you felt like I did? Sometimes it can seem like we are alone in life's arena.

Even if no one else understands our suffering, however, God does. This is not a cliché. As an omniscient he understands, of course, but this promise runs deeper than that. As I have said, God does not sit up in the stands with his arms folded like a Roman emperor watching indifferently as we suffer down in the arena. He has entered that arena voluntarily and suffered himself. He suffered for us and with us, entering into our suffering. He wasn't just stabbed to death in the Garden of Gethsemane, He suffered. He understands.

One [view] is informed by the assumption that God, if he exists, owes us a quiet comfortable life in a world free from pain. God is the divine childminder whom we should dismiss when he doesn't live up to expectations. The other view is of the Father God who passionately pursues us through the pleasure and pain that exists both with us and in the world around us. For in that world, pain and suffering are not unremitting brutal facts of existence, but things that the God of the cross and the resurrection can turn into his greatest victory.

Justin Brearley[12]

The suffering Jesus underwent was enormous. It was first of all *physical* suffering. He was homeless and had nowhere to lay his head (Lk 9:58). Leaders with power typically accumulate wealth and live in mansions—I remember travelling by boat around Seattle and seeing the mansion of one of the world's richest men, Bill Gates, overlooking Lake Washington. Jesus had no such mansion overlooking Lake Galilee. Most poignantly, he was brutally beaten, struck across the face, taunted, spat on, mocked and scourged (almost certainly with a *flagellum* made from leather thongs embedded with glass, stones or bone). He had a crown of thorns rammed onto his head and nails banged through his arms. He was lifted up on a cross and asphyxiated in a painful, exhausted state, unable to push himself up on the nails to breathe.

Jesus also underwent enormous *emotional* suffering. He was despised by the town of Nazareth, the Jewish leaders, Roman soldiers and King Herod. He was humiliated. He was rejected by his Jewish brothers, his own followers and his closest friends, who could not stay awake and suffer with him in the Garden of Gethsemane. Finally he was forsaken—or felt forsaken—by his own Father at his time of greatest suffering.

He was despised and rejected by mankind, a man of suffering,
and familiar with pain. Like one from whom people hide
their faces he was despised, and we held him in low esteem.
Isaiah 53:3

My God, my God, why have you forsaken me?
Matthew 27:46

What is perhaps most amazing is that Jesus *chose* to do all of this. He knew it would not be easy—indeed, he asked three times in the Garden if there was any other way. He was in agony knowing the level of suffering that was coming. But he chose to go ahead. What great love that is.

> **JESUS IS ONE OF THOSE RARE PERSONS WHO DOES UNDERSTAND YOUR SUFFERING**

My Father, if it be possible, may this cup be taken from me.
Yet not as I will, but as you will.
Matthew 26:39

God the Father also chose to allow his own much-loved Son to be tortured and killed. The greatest suffering I can imagine for myself is the death of one of my children. I felt the potential implications of losing a much-loved son with painful clarity when I watched the movie *Gallipoli*. This is the story of two young friends from rural Australia who volunteered together to fight in the First World War. At the climax of the movie, one of them is mowed down by machinegun fire and killed. As I left the cinema, I began to think about my two sons, both very young at the time. I imagined them going off to war and being killed by machinegun fire, dying in pools of blood. Of course I began to weep. I have close friends and patients who have lost a child and I have watched the huge burden of suffering they experience. They weep at every reminder, and there is very little consolation.

When we remember that God entered into our suffering like that, it is not a trivial thing. It means he understands whatever we are going through. After quadriplegic Joni Erickson Tada was paralysed in a diving accident, she experienced pain and discomfort from being unable to move. A friend reminded her that 'when Jesus was on the cross His back was raw from the beatings He had experienced and He must have yearned for a way to move to change positions, or shift His weight, but He couldn't'. Once she grasped that Jesus understood, Joni was better able to deal with her own discomfort.

> *He has joined us. He has hurt and played and cried and suffered. He has dignified for all-time those who suffer, by sharing their pain.*
> *Philip Yancey[13]*

> *For we do not have a high priest who is unable to empathize with our weaknesses, but we have one who has been tempted in every way, just as we are—yet he did not sin.*
> *Hebrews 4:15*

You might imagine that God doesn't understand your particular form of suffering, but he does. He is full of love and empathy. Furthermore, he takes no account of the *level* of that suffering. Jesus never says, 'Snap out of it, this is nothing. Your personal suffering might feel huge, but it is trivial compared with what I went through.' Whatever our suffering, he appreciates it as suffering. He does not use a 'suffering scoreboard' to trivialise our experiences. He understands them deeply and thoroughly.

During my time of suffering with a disabled child and a husband with terminal cancer I never really felt that [God] didn't understand what I was going through. I read the Bible again and again and realized that Jesus came as a man and experienced all kinds of suffering in life. He went through enormous emotional and physical suffering as a man. Reading about that helped me, it reminded me that he understood.

Judith Curtis

Myth: No one really understands the depth of my sadness, anguish, grief, frustration.
Promise: God does.

PROMISE 3:
JESUS LOVES YOU DEEPLY AND IS MOVED BY COMPASSION FOR YOU

In coping with suffering it is nice to know that somebody, even one person, really cares. Many people have no one. Sometimes I ask people, 'Who in your life is ever moved with compassion for you?' Some find it hard to think of anybody.

It is therefore deeply moving to know that Jesus feels such enormous compassion for us. As he enters into our suffering, he enters with tears.

When he saw the crowds, he had compassion on them, he felt compassion on them.
Matthew 9:36

Jesus wept.
John 11:35

At our deepest moments of suffering it can be hard to appreciate the love that God has for us. But we know clearly from the Bible that he does love us. He weeps as we weep. Even if no one else loves us, he is deeply moved with compassion for us every day.

> AS GOD ENTERS INTO OUR SUFFERING,
> HE ENTERS WITH TEARS AND COMPASSION

When the Lord saw her, his heart went out to her.
Luke 7:13

Jesus had compassion on them and touched their eyes.
Matt 20:34

This love can be a bit frustrating. 'If God has so much compassion for me,' we wonder, 'why doesn't he just take away my suffering? Why doesn't he heal my child?' Usually such questions remain unanswered. But regardless of our suffering, we can be assured that he loves us deeply. We cannot be separated from that love, even if we shout and rage and abuse him. As we walk through the valley of suffering, he walks with us.

Who shall separate us from the love of Christ? Shall trouble
or hardship or persecution or famine or nakedness or danger
or sword?
Romans 8:35

One of the most beautiful things about the love of God is its *unconditionality*. Again, sometimes I ask people if they have anyone in their life who loves them unconditionally. If you lost your marriage, your job, your reputation and moved to another location, would anyone still be there for you? Does the love of others depend on your staying the same, not getting depressed, keeping your family and job, behaving well?

I am often moved by the father of the prodigal son. The prodigal came home with a 'deal' for his father—to pay back his wastage of his father's money by working as a servant. His father would have none of it. He ran out and hugged him, and when his son started his well-rehearsed speech, he cut him off.

> But while he was still a long way off, his father saw him and was filled with compassion for him; he ran to his son, threw his arms around him and kissed him.
>
> The son said to him, 'Father, I have sinned against heaven and against you. I am no longer worthy to be called your son.'
>
> But the father said to his servants, 'Quick! Bring the best robe and put it on him. Put a ring on his finger and sandals

on his feet. Bring the fattened calf and kill it. Let's have a
feast and celebrate.'
Luke 15:20–23

The father's love did not depend on anything. When I talk to audiences about this story, I can barely get through the description of this unconditional love before I choke up with tears. Such love and grace shown by a dad! I hope my kids have felt some of that.

I myself have experienced God's love in many situations. In fact, when I'm in church and we sing songs about God's love, emotion wells up and I'm unable to continue singing. That experiential knowledge of God's love can only occur after you've taken the plunge and opened your mind and heart to it. Suffering is a route to that experience. Each day, when I feel my suffering, I stop and ponder the truth of his love and compassion. It is powerful for me. I avoid action-oriented thoughts that say something like 'Dear God, thank you for loving me.' Instead, I pause and think about the nature of God and his deep love for me. I stop to feel that love, remembering the feeling of the love my parents had for me when I was a child.

God's love exists whether we experience it or not, but undergoing suffering and experiencing the feeling of that love is a great way to have it embedded deep in your soul.

Praise be to the God and Father of our Lord Jesus Christ,
the Father of compassion and the God of all comfort, who
comforts us in all our troubles.
2 Corinthians 1:3–4

> **Myth:** People says things, but deep down no one is really moved with compassion for me.
> **Meditation:** Jesus looks at me in my suffering and weeps for me with a deep, abiding love.

PROMISE 4:
YOU WILL BLOOM AND GROW

We know that not everyone grows through their suffering, but God's fourth promise is that suffering will transform us, make us stronger, improve our character and give us hope. Actually, it is not the suffering itself that is the cause of growth but how we respond to it. As Charles Swindoll says, 'Life is 10% what happens to me and 90% how I react to it.' I have grown far more through hardships than when I am operating in my comfort zone.

> *Not only so, but we also glory in our sufferings, because we know that suffering produces perseverance; perseverance, character; and character, hope.*
> *Romans 5:3–4*

> *Even though our outward person is perishing, yet the inward person is being renewed day by day.*
> *2 Corinthians 4:16*

Your present circumstances don't determine where you can go; they merely determine where you start.
Nido Qubein[14]

I thank God now for how much I have grown during the time of conflict in our leadership team, though I was hurting badly at the time. I have learned so much and am now much closer to Him.
Richard Roberts[15]

Suffering can produce growth. The brokenness itself is often the foundation for blooming and change—the wounds caused by suffering are an important part of the new product.

Japanese Kintsugi cup: repaired with gold

When the Japanese mend broken objects, they aggrandize the damage by filling the cracks with gold. They believe that when something's suffered damage and has a history it becomes more beautiful.
Barbara Bloom[16]

What can this blooming look like? Here are ten ways in which you can be transformed by suffering.

You can gain greater clarity. We don't understand warmth until we have experienced cold, and we don't understand what a straight line is until we've seen a crooked one. Experiencing suffering can bring us more insight about life.

> *Something very beautiful happens to people when their world falls apart. A humility, a nobility, a higher intelligence emerges at just the point when our knees hit the floor.*
> *Marianne Wilson*[17]

You can learn to cherish. Cherishing is something deep but rare. We promise at the altar to 'love and cherish', but when I ask my friends if they actually feel cherished by anyone, they often say no. Suffering can turn that around.

> *The experience of my wife having cancer has certainly given me a much deeper appreciation for life, and for living in the present. This includes a deeper appreciation for the simple moments in everyday life and for relationships that are often taken for granted.*
> *Todd Hall*[18]

You can gain a better understanding of life's true priorities. Busyness distorts priorities. It creates short-term tyrannies that distract us from our true, deeply held goals and dreams for life.

> *[My paraplegia] was the one thing that happened in my life that I needed to have happen; it was probably the best thing*

that ever happened to me. On the outside looking in that's pretty hard to swallow, I'm sure, but hey, that's the way I view it. If I hadn't experienced this and lived through it, I likely wouldn't be here today because my lifestyle previously—I was on a real self-destructive path. If I had it to do all over again, I would want it to happen the same way.
Jerry[19]

You can become more compassionate. Compassion is uncommon in life. How many people that you know would say they feel compassion from you? Walking the journey of suffering in some strange way can make us more like Jesus in terms of compassion. And compassion can be empowering. That is a promise God gives us.

> *.... the God of all comfort, who comforts us in all our troubles, so that we can comfort those in any trouble with the comfort we ourselves receive from God.*
> *2 Corinthians 1:3-4*

You can become more comfortable with intimacy. Some people are naturally very private and struggle to share their personal issues with others. I used to be like that. Suffering can open you up to become someone who is no longer frightened of sharing their inner struggles and feelings.

> *I've always tended to discuss issues of importance, but now I am more likely to discuss more intimate things with friends and acquaintances. I am happy to go to places of personal discussion, partly because of the suffering I've experienced in my life.*
> *Todd Hall[20]*

You can become stronger, more resilient. One way that suffering can shape our character is to make us more resilient, more able to persevere. Gold is refined by fire—the heat removes impurities. The strength of character of people who have survived persecution or been prisoners of war has been written about by others and admired.

> SUFFERING SHAPES OUR CHARACTER TO MAKE
> US MORE COMPASSIONATE AND RESILIENT

During the weeks before and many months following bladder cancer surgery, I entered my own 'dark night of the soul' or 'the valley of the shadow' as I called it. It was now my turn to renew my own understandings of God when I needed Him the most. As I met with God daily and meditated throughout each day on the very words He spoke about Himself, I slowly entered a depth of intimacy with Him I didn't know existed. Richard Borg[21]

No storm, no snuggle

You can experience God's comforting presence in a special way. During a thunderstorm, young children run to their parents' bedroom, jump into bed and snuggle up to mum and dad for comfort. God our Father is also there for us in a special way during suffering. Without the storm on the Sea of Galilee during which Jesus slept, Peter would not have experienced the fear, the sinking, the cry for help and then the hand of Jesus. And we would not have read about it ever since. No thunderstorm means no fear, and no snuggles.

> *I feel like I have grown so much since my husband Paul died. During that time I don't think I would ever say that I didn't experience God's love. I felt sorry for myself at different times, but I have always felt the surety of God's hand on my life and his love. Certainly I've appreciated more about the love of God in later life, especially after Paul died of his brain tumor. I tuned into it more. Indeed to be honest, at church services I cry pretty much every time. I feel really grateful for the love of God during those times.*
> **Judith Curtis**

You can become more appreciative, more at peace and grateful. One thing I've noticed with my cancer patients is that they start to appreciate the little things in life. They talk to the butcher, the newsagent, their neighbours—people they wouldn't normally spend much time engaging with. They appreciate the trees, the grass, the sky, the ocean—they are greener and bluer than they ever noticed before. They appreciate time with people they love. In other words, they begin to appreciate things that they previously took for granted. They end up with an attitude of gratitude.

Do not worry about anything, but in everything by prayer and supplication with thanksgiving let your requests be made known to God. And the peace of God, which surpasses all understanding, will guard your hearts and your minds in Christ Jesus
Philippians 4:6

You changed my mourning into dancing; you took off my sackcloth and clothed me with gladness.
Psalm 30:12

Your faith can get stronger. Because suffering tests our faith, our faith gets stronger as we move through it and come out the other end. There are many examples of this in the Bible, ranging from Abraham, Job and other Old Testament characters through to Peter and Paul.

I know what it is to be in need, and I know what it is to have plenty. I have learned the secret of being content in any and every situation... I can do everything through him who gives me strength.
Philippians 4:12-13

When I called, you answered me; you made me bold and stouthearted.
Psalm 138:3 (NIV84)

Faith in God might not get you out of the camp, but it is enough to see you through each day.
Alexander Solzhenitsyn[22]

Suffering can make you someone more likely to influence others. Because of the strengthening of faith, hope, compassion, gratitude and the other things listed above, you may be more likely to be listened to. This is especially the case when it comes to comforting others who are going through similar pain. The Apostle Paul described how his imprisonment had actually helped him to advance the gospel (Phil 1:12–14).

> *Therefore encourage one another and build each other up,*
> *just as in fact you are doing.*
> *1 Thessalonians 5:11*

Myth: My suffering is diminishing me. I will never be the same again. "

Meditation: Suffering can cause you to grow in at least ten different ways. I encourage you to list how many of these things you have learnt through hardships.

The Diamond Prayer and Meditation

I am a very task-oriented person and I bring that to my prayers. I jump in and immediately ask God for things, including praying for people I care about, for my ministries, for my work. I have found it hard to slow down and first meditate on God, even though I know from the Bible and the model of the prophets, David and Jesus that I should do that.

Keep this Book of the Law always on your lips; meditate on it day and night, so that you may be careful to do everything written in it. Then you will be prosperous and successful.
Joshua 1:8

On my bed I remember you; I think of you through the watches of the night.
Psalm 63:6

But Jesus often withdrew to lonely places and prayed.
Luke 5:16

Through my struggles with suffering, however, I am learning to take a different approach to my daily prayers, learning to 'be still and know that he is God'. In particular, I have discovered the value of meditating on the four promises described above, each of them representing a magnificent biblical truth.

The Diamond Prayer has been a key part of that. I use the word 'diamond' because of its ability to remind me of the four key promises of Jesus for those who suffer. This kind of meditating on him is not an import from Eastern religion but an ancient Judeo-Christian practice.

Finally, brothers and sisters, whatever is true, whatever is noble, whatever is right, whatever is pure, whatever is lovely, whatever is admirable—if anything is excellent or praiseworthy—think about such things.
Philippians 4:8

But they who wait on the Lord shall renew their strength;
they shall mount up with wings like eagles; they shall run
and not be weary; they shall walk and not faint.
Isaiah 40:31 (ESV)

Let me describe it to you. I begin by taking a few deep breaths, breathing out my cares and anxieties for those moments. Then I follow the four steps of the Diamond Prayer. I imagine myself standing at the foot of the cross, and I ponder each of the four promises in turn, visualising each one as an image.

First, I look up at Jesus on the cross and let my eyes drift to his right hand. As he gently opens his fingers a little, he reveals that he is holding a diamond. This reminds me that the essential 'me' is indestructible. I ponder that indestructibility. God *promises* me that. Even when I feel like I am being crushed, I remember that God says I am like that diamond.

Second, I move my gaze back along his arm to his head and look at the crown of thorns. I note the cuts to his forehead where the thorns penetrated the skin when they were jammed onto his head and the matted blood on his face (the blood I remember during communion). I think about the enormous physical and emotional suffering he went through—he understands my suffering because he has been there. Whatever I am suffering, I meditate on the fact that God understands, completely. I do not pray, 'Dear God, thank you for understanding my suffering.' Rather, I get out of that task-mode and relax in the knowledge that he understands.

Behind the love of God lies His omniscience—His ability to 'know and understand all'… At all times, even in the midst of any type of suffering, I can realize that He knows, loves, watches, understands, and, more than that, He has a purpose. **Billy Graham**[23]

Third, I let my gaze drift down to his eyes and see tears—not tears of misery but tears because he is looking at *me*. I realise again that they are tears of compassion, because he loves me. Jesus spoke three times to others from the cross, and each time his words were full of love, not hatred or revenge—love for his mother, love for those who had hurt him and love for the repentant criminal. I ponder that deep, unconditional, unrelenting love he has for me, how moved with compassion he is for me

even though I don't deserve it. I think of how he weeps when I weep. Again, I do not turn that into a task by jumping in to thanking him for his love, but I allow it to fill my being. I remember how it felt to be loved by my parents. Then I remember that Jesus' love has the extra dimension of actually feeling compassion for me, something that one rarely feels in life.

Finally, I follow those tears as they fall to the ground below the cross and notice, to my surprise, a flower growing and blooming right where the tears are landing on rocky ground. I remember how my suffering is helping me to grow, and how, in the process, as I learn and turn my suffering into service, it is helping others to grow and bloom too. I look forward to the way my suffering will transform me in the future, helping me to grow and bloom like a flower from hard ground, and I remind myself it is his tears and compassion that have made that flower grow from unlikely ground. I also remember that my experience can potentially help other flowers to bloom and grow as I share it. Little flowers sprouting all around. I find that enormously encouraging because otherwise I can get locked into my own worries and the anxieties of the moment.

After remembering these four promises, I then pray intercessionally for specific things that are relevant to that day—for my wife, my children, the rest of my family, my friends, myself, my work and various ministries and churches. But I do that after I've had this time of mindful communion with him.

Sometimes I don't think of all four promises but focus on just one. Or I begin my prayerful meditation at the end (growth) and work backwards. Or I start in the middle. It all becomes easy as time goes on. I encourage you to try it.

This book is in some ways an example of the success of Promise 4. I have learned an enormous amount about myself and grown significantly through my experiences of suffering. My journey has also enabled me to help hundreds of others—indeed, I am now talking to you about it. I sincerely hope that you benefit from it.

> *Despite being let down by my Christian friends, I've grown so much from the abuse and trauma of my first marriage. I don't regret it because of that growth. Now I wake up every morning and I decide to have gratitude for the life that I now have and how I've grown, and I decide to be kind to people I am grateful to God for everything I have.*
> *Anonymous*

> *Twelve years have now passed since Ciara was murdered and I have finally emerged into the sunlight. But I am a different person. Tremendous growth has taken place during my long winter of exile. Ciara's death gave me new eyes through which to evaluate my own life and I'm grateful for all I have learned. If only I could've done so without Ciara's death.*
> *Never had I felt God so present in my life and so mysteriously a part of what I was experiencing. The stranglehold of grief loosened and, like a butterfly emerging from its cocoon, I emerged a different person, with a different perspective on life.*
> *Una Glennon[24]*

In the end, you can choose whether you remain in the valley of suffering and despair or begin to climb out using these four Bible-based promises. I don't say this is easy or quick. It is neither. I understand it is hard. But I do encourage you to think about this approach and embrace it.

Key points

- We shouldn't expect others to understand just how tough our suffering is.
- How we respond to suffering determines whether we grow from it.
- God makes four key promises that are helpful for surviving suffering:
  - The essential 'you' is indestructible.
  - He understands even if no one else does.
  - He is filled with compassion for us.
  - We *will* grow from our suffering.
- The Diamond Prayer reminds us to stop and meditate on those four big promises before asking God for anything.

CHAPTER 4

Practical tips
for those
who suffer

*I am certain that I never did grow in grace one-half so much
anywhere as I have upon the bed of pain*
Charles H Spurgeon

The purpose of this chapter is to provide
some understanding and practical tips for
those who are suffering to help them navigate
the journey well.

So far we have looked at suffering somewhat reflectively; now we will get very practical. In the next three chapters I want to pass on concrete ideas that have helped many people to walk through the valley of suffering and to do it well.

Every form of suffering has its own challenges, and it's not possible to deal with them all here (Part 2 looks at four different kinds in more detail). Instead I will focus on what I've learned about facing serious suffering from my personal experience of physical suffering and from what I've observed in others in my practice as a pulmonary specialist caring for people with cancer. Suffering caused by sickness is something we all have to deal with, and many of us experience it in severe forms, including terminal illness. Not everything I say here will be relevant to every form of suffering, but I hope you can draw on the ideas here to help you in whatever you are going through.

There are three stages in the journey of severe suffering. They vary with each type of suffering, can recur in cycles and can last for short of long periods. These stages are:

- finding out that you are about to suffer
- the journey of suffering
- the terminal stages

Receiving the bad news of impending suffering

Bad news is anything that tells someone they are going to suffer in ways that makes the future look dark. It could be getting a cancer diagnosis, hearing of the death of a loved one, learning they have a progressive disease like multiple sclerosis, discovering their child will be disabled or learning they need an operation or aggressive type of therapy.

Getting bad news is tough

Getting bad news is tough, and the way it is transmitted to people has profound effects. Receiving bad news in ways that lack sensitivity or empathy can make the journey harder. Examples of bad news given badly include receiving it in locations that lack intimacy (such as on a ward round, in a corridor, over the phone) or in a style that lacks empathy (such as when doctors seem to want to hurry you out of the room or use incomprehensible or insensitive language that leaves you bewildered or hurt).

My medical students have described dozens of examples of poor communication of bad news that they have seen and how they left patients weeping. It grieves me to hear such stories because we now teach medical students how to do this well, using empathic styles and words. But in the end you have little or no control over how you receive bad news, so a key is not to become disabled by any poor experience. Better to put it behind you and move on with the journey rather than being an ongoing victim of it.

After the bad news, what next?

The first step when you receive bad news about suffering is to get an idea of what lies ahead. Ignorance feeds distress, fear and a sense of losing control. To be forewarned is a great advantage rather than reacting to problems when they arise.

Many people leave a doctor's office with no clear idea what is ahead or how to manage the challenges they face. Personally I try to spend time with my patients to help them think this through. It is very helpful to understand the common physical and emotional costs and to be aware of helpful strategies for the journey of suffering, whether it be short or long.

WITH YOUR DOCTOR

Discuss the next steps. Receiving full and clear information, even when it is given in an empathic way, can be confronting, but in the end it gives you a clear roadmap for the future. It is having to guess that is hard.

Also, ask the doctor if you can continue to see them during your treatment. Breaking bad news is one of the most intimate and poignant things that a doctor does, and it is a bonding experience with a patient. Stay connected if possible—that seems to work better than just being passed around to multiple specialists.

Be aware that if the doctor is not a Christian, he/she may or may not understand all your responses.

Discuss the prognosis. You need to decide whether or not you want to know the prognosis. Not everyone does, though I find that most people want to know what it means for them long term (if it is a chronic illness) or how long they have (if it is terminal).

It can be tempting not to want to know and even to deny the problem, but I think that in general it is best to know—not necessarily at the first consultation, but soon after. I respect the right of patients to live in denial; I just don't ever see it helping much. It is short-term gain for long-term loss. But it is up to you. If you don't wish to know then make that clear.

If the illness is terminal and you do want to know, it is best to ask for simple statistics rather than a single number, that is, what is the chance that you will be alive at six months, one year, two years and so on.

UNDERSTANDING THE COSTS

Depending on the medical condition involved, the physical costs of suffering vary enormously. With cancer, for example, they may include chronic tiredness, difficulty sleeping despite tiredness, nausea, anxiety -induced palpitations, muscle tension and loss of fitness due to lack of regular exercise. Understanding the common course of a disease is vital for managing it.

Faith can feel hollow when you are suffering

Intertwined with the physical costs are the emotional ones. Initial emotional reactions include *denial* (numbness or disbelief), *anger* (commonly directed at doctors, nurses, hospitals, family or God), *depression* (realising that the diagnosis is true and feeling a sense of emptiness, resignation and darkness), *bargaining* (commonly done by believers with God) and finally *acceptance*. These represent the five stages of grief. Grief is about loss—loss of the future you imagined for yourself, activities you enjoy, relationships, laughter, intimacy, hobbies, Christian service, home-group attendance, travel. (A further discussion of grief can be found in chapter 11.)

Other emotions are also typically experienced during the suffering journey:

- **Fear** about the way things are going to turn out. This includes fear about responses to treatment, side effects and the way they might die. Christians can feel guilty if they are fearful, but I invite patients, family and friends to go ahead and feel afraid. God does not expect us to be fearless at this point—too much is at stake.

- **Sadness** at a life wasted or not yet lived. A Christian singer/songwriter named Michael Kennedy, who knew he was dying at the age of 47, said, 'It's a sad, sad thing that I will sing too few songs before my days are done.' For Christians this can be doubly hard because there are ministries to complete plus children and grandchildren who still need to be encouraged in life and faith. This is compounded if the partner without cancer is not a strong believer.

- **Regret** at time not spent with people the sufferer cares about, too much focus on work and success, not enough 'smelling of the roses'. Sadly, believers as much as non-believers can allow work to dominate their lives, and because they have a sense of divine purpose, service and 'treasure in heaven', they can postpone much of the richness of life until it is too late. Then these feelings can be overwhelming. However, such regrets can be 'paid forward' by encouraging younger people not to make the same mistakes.

Anxiety will often invade your mind when you are alone

- **Anxiety** is also common, especially worry about the impact of a serious or terminal diagnosis on family, workplace and friends. How am I going to tell them? How am I going to handle their reactions? Church communities are often warm sources of love and nurture for those with severe illness, but they can also increase anxiety. Partly this is about numbers—a lot of people you are close to know what is happening and there is less chance to 'escape' their attentions and well-meant words. It is also about expectations—if they pray that you will be healed, it is an added anxiety to come back from a doctor's visit with the news that the treatment has failed. Anxiety often arrives when you are alone, invading your mind.
- **Guilt** about behaviour that may have contributed to the illness (such as smoking, letting kids get sunburnt or moving to an area where asbestos was in the atmosphere). This can descend quickly. Christians are experts at guilt. We can easily imagine that we caused the illness by things like worry, busyness and unresolved stress or think that God is giving us what we 'deserve'.

- **Irritation and moodiness.** The above emotions can become irritating and sufferers can find themselves being easily agitated and having unusually strong thoughts about things.

You can feel lonely and that no one quite understands

- **Loneliness.** When someone has a major diagnosis of disease, they will often have many visitors early on and then few in subsequent months. This may be because friends feel uncomfortable not knowing what to say or because they get emotionally worn out. Sometimes loneliness comes from the sufferer themselves. They are too unwell or tired to maintain contact with others, or they become preoccupied with their suffering and unable to focus on others. They can feel that no one quite understands what they are experiencing. This problem is generally worse for men because they often struggle to identify and share their feelings and end up with acquaintances but no real friends with whom they can share their struggles.
- **Ongoing, disabling grief and depression.** Knowing that you will not walk your daughter down the aisle or see your grandchildren grow up is an understandable grief. Another major and very natural source of grief is that you will be leaving your partner alone. Sometimes such natural grief reactions can be so severe that it

becomes hard to get out of bed. You feel low and empty and lose interest and pleasure in things you previously enjoyed. You might have trouble concentrating, experience a change in appetite, cry a lot, and find yourself relying on alcohol and sedatives to cope or sleep. Your faith feels hollow, without warmth or passion. You can also lose motivation to take your therapy, especially if there are many drugs and you have side effects. All these emotions can be deep and feel permanent. If that is so, professional counselling/therapy may be necessary, and this in no way is a sign of your faith failing.

TELLING FRIENDS AND FAMILY ABOUT THE DIAGNOSIS

Everyone does this their own way, but first and foremost it is information that people need. This can be tiring, especially in large churches.

Doing it in writing. A simple way to avoid having to tell everyone individually (which risks exhaustion and misinterpretation) is to write a carefully worded letter. This should contain relevant information and also a bit about what you want. It could come from you, a family member or a friend appointed as spokesperson.

I used this approach myself a few years ago when my wife Jacqui found a small lump in her right breast. The doctors thought it was a cyst; I wasn't so sure, but hoped. When her biopsy came back as cancer, I needed to tell our three adult children. I did so initially by an early morning email (to avoid them having a sleepless night), giving them all the facts so they could re-read it once they stopped crying. I invited them to drop in that day and 'talk further'—of course, they all came around immediately. I was too upset myself to talk much. I don't mind crying in front of the kids, but that might have created a distraction—it was not about me. The factual letter approach made it easier for everyone.

Then I had to tell others. I did that by letter also. In the hope that you find it helpful, here is the text of what I wrote to close friends. I include it with Jacqui's permission.

Sorry to put this in writing but I need to let you know something important. Jacqui has breast cancer. She noticed a lump in her breast and had the relevant tests, including a biopsy which confirmed the diagnosis.

She is about to have surgery and chemotherapy. It has spread to lymph nodes in the armpit but no spread was found in the rest of the body on a couple of scans.

After the surgery on the breast and lymph nodes on Wednesday at Bethesda, she will need chemotherapy, some local radiation and/or other systemic therapy, depending upon receptor status. For maybe six months or more.

Jacqui has asked that this be kept fairly private until we know more and until she feels happy to pass it on at the right time, particularly to our family in the UK. Word gets around easily. So as hard as it is, please keep it to yourselves for the moment, except for partners, reminding them that it remains confidential.

She wants our life to go on as normal—events, work, visits etc. Indeed I am speaking in Sydney at a big educational leaders conference on Wednesday, staying overnight, and she doesn't want me to cancel it because it has been widely advertised, and also because other family members and friends can 'come off the bench' to help, which is what they want to do.

We are doing OK, up and down, hugs, tears, prayers, being scared and anxious, then relieved at good scan results. In the end this is just another part of our journey in life together. We are grateful not to have found out before our recent wonderful trip to England and France.

I am on my own emotional roller coaster. I think I am handling it worse than her. I have been emotionally knocked around badly by this diagnosis. This is a shock as she has no family history of cancer whatsoever and comes from a family of long-livers. Sometimes I cry, quite a bit actually, several times a day when I am alone at my desk, but mostly I just wait anxiously. I have been down this road hundreds of times with patients and their families so I know what to expect.

As always, she is being more considerate of others than thinking about herself.

I know you will share this journey with me in compassion and love. I am grateful for that. I promise to keep you informed of progress, good or bad.

Appoint a 'quarterback'. The word 'quarterback', drawn from American football, means a person who directs or coordinates. This is someone chosen by you or your family to obtain the relevant information about your suffering and pass it on to friends and your church. Without this, you or your family must keep repeating medical information, answering the same questions over and over again and having to pretend to lots of people. This is hard work. A 'quarterback' can send emails, answer questions, make phone calls or post updates online. They can also manage family tasks and any offers to help, improving the dynamics of the family and interactions with others.

Plan for the worst, hope for the best

A phrase I share with people diagnosed with cancer is 'plan for the worst, hope for the best'. This is helpful to almost every patient and family I talk to (and they have told me that often). It is a good attitude to adopt in any kind of suffering.

Hope for the best. 'Hoping for the best' means actively thinking and praying in faith for healing and a good response to therapy. I believe that God can heal miraculously—I have seen it and I have experienced it myself (I tell this story in chapter 8). 'Hoping for the best' means holding on to the possibility of a good outcome and not losing hope altogether.

On the other hand, 'hoping for the best' does not mean irrational thinking about some new treatment, getting onto aeroplanes searching for just the right faith healer or going from one healing service to another. It doesn't work that way. God answers prayers in grace, not by works. Some Christians, in chasing this elusive cure, end up feeling empty, disillusioned and sorry that they have wasted precious time. Please do not become captive to the possibility of healing and miss the opportunity for closure and 'paying it forward' to family and friends.

Plan for the worst. 'Planning for the worst' means taking account of the possibility that treatment may not ultimately be successful. I encourage my cancer patients to plan to do, within the first months after diagnosis (when they will be at their fittest), all of the things they wish to do—go to Paris, see the Taj Mahal, visit a famous natural wonder, whatever. This is not an expression of lack of faith, but of courage.

This approach is most poignant when it comes to writing letters or memoirs for children or grandchildren. These might be letters for their children to open and read after the funeral, or on their 16th or 21st birthdays, or on their wedding day. You can describe your hopes and aspirations for them, how much you love, value and admire them, and how you believe in them for the future. You are free to articulate some of the gifts that make each of them special and say how you expect them to grow and learn more and to live lives of compassion and meaning.

You also have a powerful opportunity to express your values and faith. Any child who reads, after you have died, about why you believed what you believed and how that made a difference to your life by enriching your marriage, your parenting, your friendships and your joy in service will be impacted. They might end up wanting that for themselves. I recommend that you focus on the richness of the life you have had as a Christian, not make it a gospel monologue about sin—you want them to want what you had, to be pulled magnetically towards it, not roll their eyes and be put off.

When sufferers write these kinds of letters, their tears fall on the pages. Mine would too. It is a burst of reality, because it acknowledges that they may not be there to see the future happen. I advise people not to wait until the end of the disease course to do this—by then they will be too tired or drowsy from painkillers to write. Avoidance of hard things like these is sad because it robs the children of a great gift.

Avoid avoidance

Observing the hundreds of patients I have cared for, I have noticed that those who avoid acknowledging their illness and suffering—who don't discuss it or who avoid any reminders of it—do worse. And their families do worse also.

Avoidance is a very powerful reaction. It is natural to resist talking about things that make you feel uncomfortable. Indeed, this is often a reflection of love—people are so afraid they will say the wrong thing that they say nothing. Or, since death is about grief and loss and is difficult to accept, it is easier to offer false hope ('apparently there is a new treatment in Mexico', 'I read about a patient who was healed by a fruit juice diet'). Because such reactions are reflections of love, I don't wish to criticise them. However, they often don't help the person suffering—they provide short-term comfort but in the end increase anxiety.

Don't avoid talking about your suffering or the suffering of your loved one. Here is a story of a patient of mine where avoidance was transformed into joy.

Avoiding discussing your diagnosis does not help you or your family

AVOIDANCE TURNED TO JOY

'I just want to die now. I am living in hell,' said my fifty-year-old cancer patient.

'I am sorry to hear that,' I said. 'Are you in pain?'

'No,' she said. 'But my husband is angry all day because he is stuck in the anger phase of grief, and my son couldn't stand it so he moved in with his girlfriend, which has made my husband even angrier because he says my son is now "living in sin". To add to it all, he is angry with my daughter because she drops in each evening on her way home from her hairdressing job but doesn't do anything to help; she just sits on the sofa and talks to me like she has always done, without ever mentioning the cancer. I make her cups of tea and cook her dinner in the same way I always have, and my husband thinks she should do it. I just want to die now.'

By an extraordinary 'coincidence', I went for a haircut and sensed that the lady cutting my hair might be my patient's hairdresser daughter. So I brought the subject up. She admitted she knew who I was but was clearly relieved that I was the one who mentioned it (which told me immediately she was an avoider). I arranged for the Cancer Council Family Counselling Services to visit them, and they all sat around talking about the cancer, overcoming their reluctance, holding hands and crying.

When I visited my patient in the hospice, she said, 'Bruce, I don't know what you said to my daughter but everything has been transformed. My husband is no longer angry, my son has moved back home and is helping, and my daughter is now happy to talk to me about my cancer. In fact, every week she comes in here and does my hair. Thank you so much.'

This is a clear example of a sufferer whose family's avoidance could have caused her to die badly and left the family with bitterness. But she ended up dying well. Although I don't know for sure, I would guess that the members of her family also felt that their life was in some curious way enriched by having had that intensely personal and open caring experience.

Open communication

Open communication with others is essential for navigating the journey of suffering well. It allows for understanding, support, tears and celebration.

COMMUNICATION WITH FAMILY

Discuss changes to your goals and plans with loved ones. Suffering alters plans and dreams (for example, travel, retirement, time with family). Talk together to establish new, shorter-term goals and revisit your priorities and new 'calling' (for example, spending time together, recording your life story and dreams for your kids, sharing what you are learning with your church).

Discuss changes in physical and emotional needs. Talk about needs and discuss what assistance is required, such as getting dressed, walking down stairs, washing or toileting. Partners and family members may feel uncertain about the love of the other, so reassurance may be necessary.

Prepare yourselves for daily changes, such as who does chores, pays bills, cooks, takes kids to school or even earns the family income. A person who has always been in charge may be uncomfortable becoming more dependent, or vice versa.

Avoid blame. Ongoing suffering can induce bitterness and blame directed towards others. Anger is part of the grieving process, but carers are in the firing line—we talk to young doctors about that because it can be very hurtful to be caring for a sick patient and have that patient (or more commonly their relatives) abuse you. We teach them to understand that this is a manifestation of grief and to remain kind and compassionate. As a family, choose not to be held captive to feelings of blame. Blame can lead to self-incarceration in a prison of bitterness (see chapter 11).

For those with partners, be prepared for a change in sexual intimacy. Many types of suffering affect sexual well-being. Cancer and its therapy, depression, fatigue, nausea, pain, vaginal dryness and other problems affect sex drive or sexual activity. Everyone has some level of discomfort and embarrassment talking about sexual health and intimacy, and you may need outside professional help and/or pastoral input.

COMMUNICATION WITH OTHERS

Share your difficulties without feeling guilty. Whether you are a sufferer or a carer, others typically do not know what to say, or they are afraid they will say the wrong thing and upset you. This can be hard in large communities like churches. Bring up the subject and make it clear when you don't mind talking about it and when you would rather not. Also, don't be afraid to disclose your feelings. You will soon work out who is 'safe' (those who respond with empathy) and those who are well meaning but 'unsafe' (those who respond with clichés, explanations or blame). Don't pretend that everything is OK when it is not.

Allow others to help you. Extended family, friends and church might not know how to help you, so be clear about it. Make lists and rosters. Let others know, through your 'quarterback'. Include specific chores like the laundry, shopping, washing up, walking the dog or mowing lawns.

Maintain social contact. It is easy to withdraw—indeed, that is normal if your illness is severe or even all-consuming. Your friends might wrongly assume that you do not wish to attend home group, church or social events, so inform them if you do.

Be assertive with others who are being counter-productive. If someone is well-meaning but overdoing things, talk with them and set clear boundaries. Say, for example, 'I appreciate your compassion, but to be honest we get tired and are not up to daily visits/long conversations. Can I ask you please to limit your visits to twice a week for 30 minutes? What days suit you best?'

Remember to celebrate the good times. Once honesty becomes the norm then it is easier to talk openly with family and friends. 'I may not be around for your next birthday, but hey, haven't we had some good times?' 'I remember when we... and I really appreciate the way you ...' 'Your friendship has meant a lot to me ...' Thank them for all of the things they have done for you in the past, remember good times you have shared and recall their characteristics that you have admired over the years. Laugh about the funny times.

ADDITIONAL TIPS WHEN YOU ARE STRUGGLING WITH SUFFERING

- Intentionally make some changes—change and/or re-prioritise how you live your life.
- Document your feelings—journal them, perhaps with pastoral counselling.
- Focus on blessings—it sounds trite, but intentionally reflect on all God has done for you.
- Link up with new people who will hold you up—don't fight your battle alone.
- Choose a way to serve—take the focus off yourself.

Spiritual strategies

This whole book discusses the spiritual approach to surviving the journey of suffering. The general experience of Christians who go through severe suffering is that their experience is just what the Bible says it should be—growth, insight and a deeper experience of the love of God (though not everyone feels that way).

Can I recommend that on the journey you do these four things:

1. Read about why suffering happens—you will ask that question sometimes, so it is best to think about it early (chapter 2).
2. Review the strategies for enduring and growing from suffering (chapter 3). Use the Diamond Meditation daily before you rise and at different times during the day. It has certainly changed my life and walk.
3. Review the practical tips for those who suffer and those who care for them so that you know what to expect (chapters 4 and 5).
4. Read about how to turn suffering into growth (chapters 11 and 12). This can inspire you to begin looking to the future rather than being locked into your present experience of suffering.

Prayer, too, is both a natural response to suffering and an enormously important source of strength. Prayer is heart communion with the God who is walking with you in your suffering. In addition to the Diamond Prayer, we can pour out all our thoughts, desires, questions, struggles, needs and requests to the One who understands. Prayers based on the principles discussed in this book might include:

- healing from this illness
- the professional staff involved in treatment
- the faith to believe in the best possible outcome and the courage to face up to the possibility of the worst outcome for the sake of those you love

- comfort and patience along this journey of surging emotions
- confidence in God despite the uncertainty and the explicability of this challenge
- wisdom in dealing with those who love you
- healing of broken hearts around you, including those in the past
- growth for yourself and those around you from this suffering, whatever happens
- surrender to God's will

A SUGGESTED PRAYER

Choose the parts that match your circumstance.

Heavenly Father, I feel alone, beaten up. Tears fill my eyes. I toss and turn at night.

Words can't express the ache in my heart. I feel pain every day. I am desperate for help.

I need to know that you care, that you love me. Be my refuge from pain, replacing my distress with peace, and be my strength when I feel weak and find it hard to carry on.

I'm needing some comfort right now. My heart is breaking.

My life feels kind of strange, all upside down.

My words feel like they have no strength, I have lost my confidence.

Some days I wake up and for a moment I feel happy to be alive, but this is always followed by a deep guilt for having those thoughts and I sink again.

Sorrow has kind of become a friend, a companion—ever present.

My prayer to you is that you will help grief do its work in me, and when it is done, I pray that the wound of loss will heal.

Help me not to fear the future but to boldly trust that you are in control when my emotions plunge me down, and when I am in despair.

At times when I can't talk and don't know what to say, help me to 'Be still, and know that you are God.'

Lord, I need you now more than ever.

I can no longer pretend I can help myself alone.

Be my comforter, my healer and bring me peace. Help me accept the things I can't change, give me the courage to change the things I can, and give me the wisdom to know the difference.

I don't understand you. I don't always know if I believe in you anymore.

Sometimes I feel angry, sometimes shame.

And sometimes, to tell you the truth, I feel nothing at all.

God, I'm not sure that I can do this anymore. I could use some help through these tough times. So please, place good people, kind people, along my path.

God, open my heart to you and to others, to receive help and support and love.

Please help me get some peace. Give me peace that doesn't make sense, peace that I can't produce. Give me the peace of knowing you are with me and that you love me.

(Based on Ps 46; Jn 16:33; Rev 21:4; Phil 4:6; Ps 16:8)

Facing the terminal stages

If your illness is terminal then the journey of suffering will eventually end in dying. Dying is 'normal', but there is a good way to do it and a bad way to do it.

Here I am not just talking about the sufferer but also about the family. When the dying process lacks honesty, survivors can feel cheated and be left with life-long bitterness. But when death is handled well—with honesty, laughter, celebration and tears together—the surviving family will often describe a positive effect and say, 'I am glad we handled it that way.'

Lack of honesty can affect Christians as much as non-believers. Recently a pharmacist patient of mine, a very strong Christian, died having spent six months in complete avoidance. He never talked to his teenage kids about the fact he was dying. Although at his funeral someone described this as 'showing the kids how brave he was', I thought the opposite.

You may be healed or God may be saying to you, 'Well done, good and faithful servant, your time on earth is up.'

I sometimes think that lack of honesty and the resulting avoidance is like seeing a black door in the house and walking past it all the time, afraid to go through it, afraid of what is on the other side. If a person does get to the point where they are able to grasp the handle, turn it, open the door and walk through, to their surprise they can enter a garden. In that garden there is a lot of expressed love, and they see that the sky is bluer and the trees greener than they have noticed before, and that, because every day is a gift, they can live the rest of their life with gratitude. That is not to say they won't suffer physically or emotionally in the process, but they will have discovered the secret that to a large extent makes the difference between dying badly and dying well.

For Christians it is important to understand that dying is not a defeat of faith. If God is saying, 'Well done, good and faithful servant, it's time to come home to me', accept it and die well, die magnificently, with courage, kindness and grace.

(Further thoughts about managing terminal illness can be found in chapter 7.)

This chapter has focused on severe suffering from illness, but I encourage you to apply the principles to whatever you're going through. Remember that your suffering does not have to own you. I acknowledge that walking through suffering well and growing from it can be hard, so I send you hugs in whatever stage you're at in the journey.

Key points

- Your suffering does not have to own you.
- Suffering often brings a rollercoaster of emotions including disbelief, anger, guilt, depression, fear and regret.
- Don't guess—identify the strategies that will help you get through your suffering.
- Loneliness is a risk—don't let yourself become reclusive.
- Avoid avoidance—tell friends and family everything, in writing if that is easier.
- Plan for the worst and hope for the best (which can sometimes include supernatural healing).
- Understand what 'dying well' means compared with 'dying badly'.

CHAPTER 5

Practical tips for those who care for sufferers

Some days there won't be a song in your heart. Sing anyway.
Emory Austin

> The purpose of this chapter is to provide some understanding and practical tips for those closest to people who suffer so that they are not crushed by the burden of care.

When discussing the costs of caring, I emphasise the joy and growth that can flow from it. Despite the costs, most carers find the role rewarding and a time of great personal growth. Certainly, for a Christian, caring can be a road to growth, transformation and the learning of perseverance. Being there for others can create strong relationships and fond memories (often appreciated most when the time of caring has ended). Have you felt these things when you have cared for others?

Carers can burn out

On the other hand, carers always pay a price. They are often forgotten as attention is focused on the victims of suffering. If there are joys in caring, these joys are typically tempered with physical and emotional demands. Christians pay this price too. There is no escape.

There are different sorts of carer roles. Examples of carers include:

- family of those who suffer (partners, children, siblings, parents)
- close friends and communities of sufferers (churches, home groups, workplaces)
- those who serve at the coalface of suffering (pastors, doctors, social workers, missionaries, police, support group volunteers, chaplains and many more)

To aid understanding, I will first discuss some of the major costs of caring. I will then give some tips on managing them that will be relevant in different ways for each of the roles mentioned above.

The costs for carers

THE COSTS FOR CLOSE CARERS

Close carers who have frequent, perhaps day-to-day contact with someone who is suffering may be called on to provide many forms of support—physical, emotional, psychological, social and spiritual. They have a front row seat on the person's journey of suffering. The price paid by close carers can be high. It can include:

Anger and frustration are common

Anger and frustration. Caring can produce anger and frustration because your life is disrupted, you struggle to juggle family responsibilities and work, you are confused and you have lost control of your life. You feel trapped. Frustration with other family members and friends who you think should help more, or who say unhelpful things, is common. This can be extra hard for Christians because of the higher expectations we place on each other to be compassionate and thoughtful. It is also frustrating to deal with often unpredictable mood changes in the person suffering, especially if they are self-absorbed and do not seem to appreciate your work and sacrifice or ever say thanks.

Guilt. Carers feel guilty about their anger and frustrations, about not saying or doing the right things, about being healthy and not suffering themselves, and about not doing a good job of caring. If they take a break they also feel guilty. This is especially an issue for Christians, who have a high bar when it comes to what love looks like (1 Corinthians 13).

Physical and emotional exhaustion are common in all carers

Exhaustion. This is common in carers, but there is guilt about letting on just how tired you are. The combination of extra roles, lack of sleep, worry and having to respond to questions from others inevitably takes a huge toll. Sometimes exhaustion is not so much physical as emotional. You don't get a break from your worries and feelings. Burnout is a risk.

Feeling overwhelmed. Caring for someone can be overwhelming. It is easy to feel that you don't know what to do—or what *not* to do. Some carers lose confidence in themselves. It is easy to over-worry about the sufferer, the results of tests and your own journey—how you will cope, what the future holds, finances and loneliness.

Overdoing caring. If you are the main carer you may overdo things. Sometimes carers generate meaning from their caring because of their love for the sufferer, or in some cases (such as adult children) because it is a way to repay the sufferer for years of neglecting them. Overdoing caring is a particular issue for Christians, whose consciences have been shaped by the example of the Good Samaritan. Carers may try to become experts in the medical journey and the drugs. They may try to dominate discussions with medical staff and control the flow of information to family and friends. They may become overprotective. It is their expression of love, but it isn't always helpful.

THE SPECIAL COSTS FOR CHILDREN IN A CARING FAMILY

These emotional and physical responses when someone in a family is suffering are not felt just by adults but also by children. Sometimes jealousy and embarrassment are added in. These feelings can be 'internalised' and not obvious, so being aware of this is an important step in taking care of children. They may want to 'do the right thing', to help those who are helping the sufferer. They may face school or social issues such as being less available to friends. They may sacrifice their own interests and neglect their own issues.

Children of sufferers can 'internalise' their concerns

Children can also experience 'parentification', taking on responsibilities similar to parents' and no longer behaving like children.

In the process of caring for someone who is suffering, the needs of children can be overlooked ('What about me?'). It is easy for them to feel neglected and unimportant. They may have many questions that are unanswered because the parents are trying to shield them, and in those situations their imagination takes over.

THE COSTS FOR MEDICAL AND OTHER 'COALFACE' CARERS

For frontline carers like doctors, pastors and social workers, caring can also take a serious toll. Helen Roseveare was an English doctor who worked in the Congo during the country's bloody 1960s rebellion, showing sacrificial love despite being repeatedly beaten and raped by soldiers. When she first arrived, she was appalled by the number of sick patients needing attention and disappointed that the staff closed the clinic at around 6 pm. She decided to keep it open, working until late in the evening. After a week or so, she was utterly exhausted and wanted to give up. Her compassion had led to overwork.

Many of my colleagues in medicine have stumbled over this problem, neglecting their families and their own well-being out of a misjudged sense of duty and compassion. In the process, some have even ended up depressed and divorced. A couple of years ago I noticed that tendency in myself, so during winter I headed north to a warmer climate, camping, sitting around a campfire and staring at the ocean. It was better than any anti-depressant drug.

We will always be surrounded by people with needs, some of them great. Without good self-care, 'coalface' carers will be unable to help any of them. Carers need to give themselves permission to get refreshed and stay strong (without/despite feeling, guilty about it).

Self-care for carers

If carers burn out it doesn't help anyone. Yet carers' pain is often a neglected area in the expression of love for those who are suffering. It can be almost as difficult, if not as difficult, for the loved ones of someone who is suffering as it is for the sufferer themselves. It is especially hard for partners.

If you are caring for someone who is suffering, the main thing you need is to give yourself permission to care for yourself as well.

I confess that I let myself down in this regard far too often. But when my wife was suffering from depression, I was encouraged to take a lesson from surf lifesaving. When someone is in trouble in the water, you swim over to help hold them up while awaiting rescue, but you need to be careful that in their panic they don't drag you under so that you both drown. You must be willing to let go and swim away for a minute to regain your strength, then come back and hold them up again—otherwise you both run the risk of going under.

> **CARERS CAN BURN OUT AND THAT DOESN'T HELP ANYONE. TAKE CARE OF THEM TOO**

At times it takes someone else to liberate carers from the pressure or guilt. I recently visited a friend who had just left hospital following a cancer operation. After he left the room to attend to something, I asked his wife how she was travelling. They live near the coast, but she said that whenever she went for her usual walk along the beach, she felt guilty leaving her husband at home. I shared the lifesaver example that had helped me. She was very encouraged and appreciated getting 'permission' to look after herself so that she could better 'hold up' her husband.

Jesus himself often took time out despite being surrounded by never-ending needs and opportunities that he could have been attending to (for example, Luke 5:16). Rather than feeling guilty about self-care, carers need to embrace it as essential.

TIPS FOR SELF-CARE FOR CARERS

- **Spend time with people** you care about, or who provide a friendly environment, especially (though not exclusively) in your church community. Do this even if you feel like retreating completely.
- **Get active,** even though you may not feel like getting out of bed.
- **Embrace and face any grief** associated with the role of caring. For example, every week I get a coffee in our building's coffee shop and deliberately sit in the chair I was sitting in when I got the news that my wife had cancer and I wept. I 'get back on the horse'. Allow yourself to feel any emotions associated with your role as a carer.
- **Don't fake it.** Be honest with your family, friends and church community.
- **Write your experiences down** to help you process them.
- **Find places of joy and laughter.**
- When you can, **turn your grief into help for others**.

DON'T AVOID SEEKING HELP

It's important not to avoid seeking help from a counsellor, pastor or other professional, or from relevant support groups (including any home group) that provide a chance to talk, share and get advice.

Don't be afraid to ask for professional counselling. This is not an admission of failure, nor should it be a source of guilt. If you love the person you are caring for, getting help may be an expression of that love since it means you will be able to care for them better. Similarly, consider accessing the support services that are available. Carer Support Groups encourage carers to come together on a regular basis to discuss their situation, socialise, share information and ideas, and offer each other support.

Apart from formal counselling, there are other ways you can look after yourself. These include:

- **Relaxing with family and friends.** On my trip working in Aceh after the 2004 tsunami, the team retreated each Sunday afternoon to the beach. I initially felt guilty because there was so much devastation and so many medical needs that it seemed inappropriate to be frolicking. It was a naïve and ill-informed view—the team needed that break to avoid burnout.
- **Organising respite services** for the person you care for.
- **Taking time out** for yourself for things like relaxing, reading, the movies, hobbies and exercise—even going away on a break.

USE SOCIAL MEDIA

In social media, modern technology has given us an excellent tool for getting emotional support.

'Thank you for coming to help us'

I have not been a great user of social media, but on a medical relief team after the 2018 Sulawesi earthquake, I became utterly exhausted. During the Sunday afternoon break I was really low and felt like giving up and going home. I sent some text messages to family and close friends, but as I did it, I looked at the blue F on my phone and thought, 'Hey, that's what Facebook is about—friends and family communicating with each other.' So I worked out how to send a short message saying where I was and attached my favourite photograph from the trip—a grateful old lady in a disaster relief camp who gave me a hug to say, 'Thanks for coming to help us.' Overcoming my reluctance because a small percentage of people might think I was 'big noting' myself, I posted it. It was wonderful to receive encouraging feedback from friends and extended family over the next few hours. I can't tell you how much it lifted my spirits. I realised that this was a situation in which social media really works.

Such sharing is good for the sharer ('a problem shared is a problem halved') and reduces the risk of burn out, accumulated stress, depression and PTSD. It is also good for the recipients to know where you are at, what your needs are and how you are feeling, and to have the opportunity to support you in difficult moments. I know that things like Facebook groups for sufferers with different medical conditions and WhatsApp friendship and prayer groups have been enormously helpful to many.

Personal compassion fatigue

When suffering is prolonged, it is not unusual for 'compassion fatigue' to set in. You run out of time and energy to keep helping. The church will rally around someone who has cancer, bringing meals and making contact, but when the suffering is chronic, such attention can fade away. That is to be expected to some extent. It is when it disappears altogether that people feel abandoned.

I have had to learn a lesson here in my own practice as a carer. Because I have cared for hundreds of individuals who have been suffering and for their carers, I tend to temper my initial response a bit so that I don't get worn out too early. I want to be able to continue providing care over the journey. Becoming aware of compassion fatigue might be a sign that you need more support.

Caring for the carers

During a consultation with a patient who is dying of cancer, I will at some stage turn to the partner and ask, 'How is it going for you?' They will typically reply, 'It's tough, but we're getting through it with the help of family and friends.'

I then offer them a second opportunity to say how it *really* is for them. 'That's great,' I say, 'but in my experience of hundreds of situations like this, it's often as hard for the carer as it is for the person who is suffering, so I just thought I'd check.'

At that point, two things commonly happen. First, the carer will begin crying because it is the first time that someone has understood and empathised with just how hard it is caring for someone who is dying. Second, the patient will turn to the carer with a look of surprise—they have never thought of how hard it is for their loved one to care for them so much (out of kindness the carer has usually never let on just how hard it is for them).

Carers can't do it all alone. It helps enormously if those who are around them, their family, friends and church communities, understand the pressures and pain that can be involved in caring. They gain strength when others express kindness towards them and don't just focus on the person who is suffering.

If you are a carer, please don't try to soldier on blindly in your journey of caring. There is a 'best practice' in doing that journey which provides a suite of potentially helpful tips to think about. I encourage you to think through those mentioned in this chapter and discuss them together as loved ones.

Key points

- Caring closely for those who suffer is a joy but can itself have profound impacts.
- Realise that carers always pay an emotional and physical price for caring.
- Don't feel guilty about caring for yourself.
- Be aware that the children of sufferers pay a special price.
- Don't be afraid to ask for professional counselling.
- Personal compassion fatigue might be a sign you need more support.

CHAPTER 6

Practical tips
for friends and churches

My son's drug addiction is very public and I just can't face having to answer everybody's questions all the time, even though they are well-meaning and want to help. But I really appreciate it when friends ask me how I am doing rather than how my son is doing.

Anonymous

> The purpose of this chapter is to provide suggestions on how to respond to those who suffer and their loved ones. We know we can make things worse rather than better by what we say and do or what we *don't* say and do. To know how to respond best is to know how to help rather than hurt.

Several years ago, when my wife was undergoing treatment for breast cancer, I began to leave our church services just as the leader announced the final song. I would often run into a friend leaving at the same time, a lawyer whose daughter was undergoing intensive therapy for a life-threatening bone marrow condition. We joked that it was like the 'two-minute warning' given towards the end of a sports game.

We discovered that we were both leaving early for the same reason—to avoid being asked the same questions over and over again by well-meaning friends. I feel a bit guilty saying this because people wanted to express their concern, but I found that it became tiring and, in the end, irritating. Being asked 'How is Jacqui?' once or twice was OK, but it was impossible to answer that question 20 or 30 times. It was especially hard because it was my wife they were talking about, yet it was a very hard journey for me too. To be honest, I didn't really want to keep talking about it. It would have been easier if someone had said, 'Hey Bruce, it's always hard for the caring partner—how are *you* going?'

Another friend whose wife had breast cancer had a similar experience. At the time when she was undergoing therapy, he was at one big church event where he was relentlessly bombarded with the question 'How is your wife?' He told me how it made him feel and I could not get the image out of my head: 'I felt like I was standing in a field being relentlessly pecked by crows, but I had nowhere to go.'

This is one of the most important chapters of this book. It contains specific tips to enable us to turn our compassion for those who are suffering, and those who care for them, into words and actions that are helpful rather than useless or worse. So often we feel sad for people and mean well but say the wrong thing. I have done so many times.

Christian communities and suffering

It is understandably hard for families, friends and church members to know what to say and do to help those who suffer. That can be frustrating. Christian communities can be wonderfully supportive and helpful, but sadly they can also act with good intentions that end up being inappropriate and hurtful. Unfortunately, loving God, feeling worshipful and being moved with compassion do not automatically translate into supportive words and actions.

Churches are not alone in this. The majority of health professionals, when initially exposed to sick patients, also don't feel comfortable talking about suffering with them, so it is not unreasonable for those with less experience at dealing with human suffering to feel awkward and make mistakes.

> CHURCH COMMUNITIES NEED TO LEARN
> TO CHANNEL THEIR COMPASSION INTO WORDS
> AND ACTIONS THAT ARE HELPFUL

I remember crying at the chapel ...
People just didn't know what to say to me or to Kent's parents.
Bill Gates[25]

Church members can learn how to best express their love

In this chapter I will talk about some of those mistakes. I am not trying to be critical—I have made these errors myself. I understand how the combination of compassion and uncertainty can make anyone uncomfortable and can lead to saying unhelpful things. I used to wish I knew what to say. I bet you do too.

Church communities, which are families, need to learn how to channel their compassion into words and actions that are helpful, not hurtful. A key to this is to be Jesus-like in our communication with those in need.

The five features of Jesus-like engagement

How Jesus' style of engagement can inform our care of sufferers and those who care for them is a key principle underlying the strategies described in this book, so it will be helpful to delineate what that looks like. I add some personal examples of how this Jesus-style has changed the way I respond to those in need.

THE FIVE FEATURES OF JESUS-STYLE ENGAGEMENT

- Listening before speaking
- Compassion
- Words followed with action
- Responding to need, not status
- Fearlessness

1. Listening before speaking. One of the interesting things about many of Jesus' interactions was how he listened first to understand a person's issue before speaking. That was true even if the issue was obvious, such as blindness (Mk 10:46–52), leprosy (Lk 5:12–16) or spiritual challenges (Matt 19:16–22). He didn't speak with the same 'formula words' to everyone.

James 1:19 says, 'Let every person be quick to hear, slow to speak.' Each sufferer will have a specific issue that concerns them, and listening enables you to respond to that issue.

> *A neighbour of mine who was in the terminal stage of cancer visited me to chat. Instead of jumping in and doing my normal doctor thing of explaining to him what the end stages would be like, I chose to ask him if there was anything he was afraid of. I wanted to listen to him, to his heart. He said his biggest fear was that his young children would be forever damaged by his early death. If I hadn't listened, I would not have had a chance to help him die in peace regarding that deep concern.*

2. Compassion. The eye-witness accounts of Jesus in the Gospels often refer to his being moved with compassion (Matt 9:36; 14:14; 15:32; 20:34;

Mk 6:34; 8:2; Lk 7:13). What do you think people saw that made them note that in later descriptions of the interactions? I bet it was a combination of tears and body language.

> ## KNOWING THE 'JESUS STYLE' CAN CHANGE THE WAY YOU RESPOND TO THOSE IN NEED

In chapter 3 I mentioned how I sometimes ask people if they have anyone in their life who is moved with compassion for them. Most have few or no such people. Christians are called to be people moved by compassion for those in need—to be Jesus to them.

Not long ago I ran into a young doctor whose marriage had broken up. As I sat listening to her, I felt sad for her and started to weep. I am more of a 'get on and solve the problem' kind of person, but I understand how God asks me to show compassion, and his spirit has softened my heart to do so. In the end, though, it is still a choice whether to demonstrate Jesus-like compassion or not.

3. Words followed with action. No one could accuse Jesus of being one of those people who are all words and no action. He responded, usually immediately. He alluded to the problem of form without action in the parable of the Good Samaritan (Lk 10:25–37). Sadly, many Christians will speak to and pray for someone in need, but not act. That is not Jesus-style engagement.

I was at a major international cricket match one day and visited a friend in a corporate box. During that visit I began chatting to another corporate leader, who dropped a hint that he had had a tough year. When I asked him if he meant tough with his company or personally, he said personally. We were interrupted, so the conversation ceased. But the next day I felt moved to contact him and ask if he wanted to grab a coffee and talk about it. He

*invited me to lunch and told me that his marriage was collapsing badly. I'm
so grateful for the Jesus model of following up with actions, and we have
remained close ever since.*

4. Responding to need, not status. It is impressive that Jesus' interaction
with others was independent of their status. He engaged with leaders and
lepers with the same focused attention (Matt 8:1–13). Sometimes I imagine
Jesus being at a party with the rich and famous and talking to the waiters
with exactly the same interest and compassion as he talked to the guests.
Most of us would either focus on the rich guests or resent them and eulo-
gise the poor. Jesus responded to everyone equally as people made in the
image of God.

*Once at a funeral I was talking to the most powerful health minister in the
country. I was just about to 'strategically' let her know about a new medical
research program we were developing when I was tapped on the shoulder by
a factory worker who wanted to talk to me about his fears of asbestos in his
workplace. I really wanted selfishly to continue talking to the health minister,
but I had a sudden realisation that Jesus would stop and turn to this man, be
moved with compassion for him and talk to him. That's what I did. The health
minister moved off to talk to others.*

5. Fearlessness. Jesus did not shy away from hard questions (for example,
when talking with the woman at the well in John 4). He approached them
gently but clearly, and without fear. When you talk to someone who is
suffering, it is easy to try to avoid personal discussions. But to speak gently,
respectfully and compassionately to sufferers about the hard issues, when
appropriate, is to be Jesus-like. Don't be tyrannised by the notion that they
will hate you for it.

*By nature I am a bit shy, and certainly would never consider asking people
personal questions. But my experience with sufferers and their families has*

taught me that it is important to do so, provided it is done appropriately. Most people don't have anyone who is willing to engage with them about the deep issues that are troubling them—we tend to change the subject, trivialise things or make a joke. Jesus-like care means being willing to go to those hard places.

I have learnt the '98/2 rule'—98% of those you engage with in this way will love that you did so while 2% will react negatively. If you worry that someone will be in that 2%, you are not loving the sufferer like Jesus did but loving your-self and what people might think of you. In the process you will be denying the 98% the chance of deep, meaningful discussion about things that really worry them. (And to be honest, most of that 2% later express appreciation for the concern shown, even though they reacted at the time)

Taking 'the leap': how friends and church members can best respond to suffering

When asked by churches how they can show compassion to someone in their congregation who is suffering, I condense the five features of Jesus-style interaction into one word: LEAP.

L — Listen

E — Empathise

A — Act

P — Pray

The LEAP

LISTEN

Being a good listener is rare. After social functions, Jacqui and I often estimate the percentage of people who genuinely listened to us—our normal count is 5% or less. That means 95% or more do not genuinely listen or show any interest by asking questions. Other friends state similar observations.

Would you be described as a good listener?

There is enormous power in listening. After a severe backyard accident with a circular saw that landed me in hospital for several weeks (see chapter 8), I was still in agonising pain on the day I was discharged. That evening a close Christian friend came to visit me and asked how I was doing. As I told him how much I enjoyed being home but was disappointed to still be in such pain, I found myself sobbing. Rather than trivialise my situation ('You'll be OK') or explain it ('That's just happening because …'), he listened to me as I talked it through, showing empathy rather than feeling a need to talk. I have found in my life that some Christians have a special way of doing that.

Anyone can learn to be a better listener. Here are some things you can do:
- Resist the urge to speak. You don't *have* to say things.
- If you don't know what to say, be honest and admit, 'I wish I knew what to say.' Avoid blurting out things that are unhelpful or hurtful.
- Feel free to leave long silences—really long ones if necessary. Don't feel obliged to fill the space with words.
- Let others talk when they want to.

Later in this chapter I list examples of words that are either helpful or unhelpful.

EMPATHISE

Empathy is a beautiful way to express compassion. It involves being able to sense and understand other people's thoughts and feelings.

Rejoice with those who rejoice, weep with those who weep.
Romans 12:15

Empathy is about allowing time (not looking as though you can't wait to get away) and about body language (for example, making eye contact at eye level). It is also about appropriate touch, Such as putting your hand on a forearm or shoulder, or giving a hug. Touch is vital for humans—every child seeks hugs when they are sad or in pain.

> **TEARS ARE A WONDERFUL NATURAL WAY OF COMMUNICATING COMPASSION AND EMPATHY**

Empathy is also about tears. A preparedness to cry with someone is wonderfully empathic. A moment ago I mentioned a young doctor I ran into who was having marriage difficulties (I knew her a little from church circles). Since we were outside a coffee shop at the time, I asked if she would like to have coffee with me. As she told me her story, I had no helpful answers for her but found myself weeping—for her in her dilemma and agony, for her husband, for her family, and for the church navigating the journey between compassion and the risk of being perceived as judgmental. We finished our coffee and I gave her a hug, but wondered if I'd done anything to help her. A month later, I was in another coffee shop when a middle-aged couple tapped me on the shoulder and asked, 'Are you Bruce Robinson?' It was the young woman's parents. The mother told me that my tears and nonjudgmental empathy had given her daughter a wonderful boost. She had immediately gone to her mother's office and they had wept together.

You can learn words of empathy, but tears are natural and unforced. Many Christians worry that if they are also praying for the person, tears might suggest a lack of faith, as if to say, 'Even though I am praying, I don't really believe my prayer will change anything.' But don't worry—what tears actually say is 'I really care about you and what you are going through.'

Obviously, your empathy for those who suffer needs to be independent of their status. To care for someone who doesn't think they are worthy of anyone's attention is a beautiful, Jesus-like thing to do.

ACT

Suffering can be a lonely journey. Despite the compassion of friends, avoidance is common, and this includes people failing to act in ways that could have been helpful. It can be tricky—you don't want to invade a person's space when they are tired and suffering, but you don't want to avoid the possibility of helping altogether.

Don't avoid friends, even imperfect ones

One of the keys is 'being there'. This is fundamental for all human relationships, whether it is marriage, parenting or friendship. Ask yourself, 'Whom do I know who will always be there for me, through thick and thin?' If we are to be like God, this is one unarguable characteristic—to always be there for someone you care about.

> *God has said, 'Never will I leave you; never will I forsake you.'*
> **Hebrews 13:5**

This is a particularly poignant issue for those who suffer. I have often heard sufferers say, 'I found out who my real friends were. I have since drifted away from some friends and made close new ones.'

Later in this chapter is a checklist of actions to consider.

> **AVOIDANCE IS COMMON AND INCLUDES A FAILURE TO SPEAK OR ACT IN WAYS THAT COULD BE HELPFUL**

PRAY

Praying as a home group or church is obvious. Offering to pray with those who suffer can be wonderfully caring. But it can also be empty and clichéd if the prayer is used as a replacement for words of empathy and acts of compassion.

Prayer is not about trying to fix the problem with enough praying, and it is not about finding the right words. It is about calling out to a loving and powerful God in your distress (Ps. 102)—asking, like Jesus in Gethsemane, if this time of trial can possibly be avoided, yet surrendering.

Ask them what they would like you to pray for

Ask the person who is suffering about their main concerns and what specifically they would like you to pray for. Resist the urge to provide answers and theology in your prayers. When you know you will be talking to someone who is suffering, you could write these words on the back of your hand: *Not about me; be cliché-free.*

Not about me. Listen. It's not about you and your feelings, your analysis. *Be cliché-free.* Resist the urge to deliver biblical clich*é*s. Just be there.

> *The ministry team from church came and prayed for [Paul] and laid on hands. But no one told him that they knew he would be healed. Those prayers may have given us the extra time and for that I am grateful. Indeed he lived for three and a half years free of symptoms, much longer than the six months or so that was originally predicted, and we appreciated that time. Certainly Paul and I were grateful for the care shown by that prayer given to us by the ministry team.*
> *Judith Curtis*

Disability and suffering and I exist for the glory of God. I pray that in times of suffering and times of pleasure, my life would magnify the One who 'died for all, that those who live might no longer live for themselves but for him who for their sake died and was raised'.
Joe Eaton

The suggestions for ways that sufferers can pray in chapter 4 can easily be adapted for use in praying for/with them.

Tips about what to say and do

People who suffer need love, not a bucketful of verses, guesses or perceived logic. Don't be the clanging cymbal of 1 Corinthians 13.

I was at a funeral recently of a Christian friend. One man couldn't stop spouting biblical clichés to me, his friend. It was awful. But another person then just sat with me saying nothing. That was just what I needed, and he knew it.
Anonymous

UNHELPFUL THINGS NOT TO SAY

- Don't say anything that puts the focus on you and your feelings.
  'I know how you feel.'
  'I am devastated.'
  'I can't think straight.'
  Expressing anticipatory grief by talking about your sadness and how much you would miss them.
  Your own observations such as 'you've lost so much weight' or 'you don't look unwell.'
- Don't offer spiritual pressure, explanations and clichés.
  'You need to pray more', 'God has a reason for this' and other Christian clichés. Unwarranted explanations.
  Over-spiritualising (for example, quoting unhelpful verses).

Well-meaning but generally unhelpful phrases

'God must have wanted your spouse/child/friend back in heaven.'
'You should get to a place of giving thanks.'
'You will become an example to others.'
'You didn't pray enough.'
'You must have a hidden sin.'
'You need more faith and less reliance on doctors.'

- Don't present any uncertainty as a certainty.
  'I am sure it will be fine.'
  'You don't need to worry.'
  Giving certainty where only uncertainty exists (for example, 'I had a word from God that you will definitely be healed.' Keep that to yourself.).
  'I heard on TV about a new diet that cures cancer.'
  'I'm sure the doctors have it wrong because you are young and healthy, you exercise, you have a wonderful ministry and your kids need you.'
  'Just keep a positive mental attitude and you will be healed.'
  'I read something on the internet that your doctors seem to be keeping from you as they haven't mentioned it.' (Passing on things like that might make you feel like you are helping, but it is often quite selfish and more about the speaker than the person suffering. Remember, doctors spend years studying—and in any case, just because information is on the internet does not mean it is either true or wise.)

- Don't say anything that trivialises or dismisses the illness.
  'Just get over it.'
  'It's time to move on.'
  'You're just attention-seeking.'
  'Time to pull yourself together.'
  'Snap out of it.'
  'It's all in your mind.'
  'Everyone has bad days/weeks.'
  'Just stop feeling sorry for yourself and smile more.'

'It's a good thing you already have two healthy kids.'

Comparing the sufferer to someone worse off to downplay their condition.

Making lame jokes to avoid discussing the suffering.

Always changing the subject to something trivial because you are uncomfortable.

'Weaponising' Romans 8:28 to say that the person's suffering is good. (It is not good, and that verse does not say it is. It says that God can make something bad work for good in the future. Right now, it is just plain bad.)

- **Don't say anything that 'boomerangs' back to your story.**

  'Now you know how I feel.'

  'Hey, I once had something similar.'

  'My brother had this.'

  'Welcome to my world.'

- **Don't say, 'I understand.'**

  You won't entirely understand, even if you think you've been on a similar journey yourself. Better to try to understand how the other person is feeling in their journey. It might be helpful to say you have been down a similar path so you understand a little, but seek to understand how it is for them.

- **Don't give unhelpful 'explanations'.**

  We seem to have an urge to jump in too early to tell people why they are suffering, ranging from suggesting the cause to speculating on the potential spiritual benefits. Even Job did not get an explanation from God for his suffering, and if anyone 'deserved' one, he did.

- **Don't use 'should' language.**

  You 'should'... pray... eat... not eat... go... read... try...etc.

- **Don't avoid the truth.**

  Speaking words means not avoiding the truth, not letting your fear of making a mistake or feeling bad yourself cause you to avoid the subject. Jesus never showed such fear, and we need to be willing to feel uncomfortable and take a gentle, compassionate risk when talking to those who suffer.

HELPFUL THINGS TO SAY

- 'Thanks for sharing your pain so honestly.'
- 'I am sorry this has happened to you.'
- 'I feel sad and I grieve with you and your family and am praying for you.'
- 'I don't really understand, but if it is OK to ask, please help me understand.'
- 'I will be there for you.'
- Be sensitive to overloading the person.
- Ask if there is someone who is 'quarterbacking' the information and passing it on to the church so that you can rely on that person rather than repeatedly asking the person who is sick.

UNHELPFUL THINGS NOT TO DO

- Don't pray instead of visiting.
- Don't find yourself too busy all of a sudden to visit.
- Don't use the 'I don't know what to say so I'll avoid visiting and making things worse' excuse.
- Don't use 'faith' to avoid the reality and discomfort of the problem. Not everyone is healed—some are, some are not. Faith can sometimes be a strategy to avoid facing the reality of life and our own responsibility to act within that reality. Irrevocable belief that suffering will go away is wonderful, but it can also masquerade as a more spiritual response than compassionate listening and empathy, especially considering that not everyone is healed.

- Don't outstay your welcome if you visit. Ask what works best for them. Sometimes it is best to just leave the food on the doorstep.
- Don't simply say, 'Is there anything I can do to help?' That usually leads to nothing.

HELPFUL THINGS TO DO

- Ask what specific things you can do by giving examples.
- Perhaps you could list these in writing to leave with the sufferer or their family to tick anything they think they might like and then return the list to you.
- Create a roster of other willing helpers.
- Pick up the kids from school, take them to the playground or library, or just babysit.
- Do stuff around the house such as the laundry, walking the dog, mowing the lawn, gardening or filling up their car with fuel.
- Offer to attend the clinic or chemotherapy session with them or pick up their prescriptions—my wife found this a great time to catch up with friends.
- Help with a roster to bring them some soup or dinner.
- Help them pull together a memoir photo album for their children and grandchildren.
- Sometimes friends will shave their heads during chemotherapy, or wear wigs, in solidarity.

How church members can care for carers too

*Carry each other's burdens, and in this way you will fulfill
the law of Christ.*
Galatians 6:2

In most situations of suffering, almost all attention is focused on the
sufferer. But carers, typically family members and friends, also suffer.
They can find the caring hard work and can themselves pay a high price
for trying to help. In some studies, for example, 75% of couples dealing
with chronic disease end up divorced, and a significant percentage of acci-
dent/disaster first-responders suffer symptoms of post-traumatic stress
disorder (PTSD).

Understanding how to support carers, whether they are family/friends
or communities such as churches, is an important goal of this book (see
chapter 5). I have found that continued care for carers does not have to be
time- or emotion-intensive but is more a reflection of just being there for
them, caring enough to remember their situation and asking how things
are going in an empathic way. It is often just a matter of a text message,
a coffee or a trip together to a sporting event. By writing them into my
Outlook calendar, I get reminders that my self-absorbed self would otherwise forget.

The simplest way to care for carers is to follow the LEAP steps described above.

- **Listen.** Usually everyone's focus is on the sufferer. Focus on listening to the carer.
- **Empathise.** I find in my medical practice that appreciating carers' difficulties gives them permission to be honest and describe their struggles.
- **Act.** Take them out somewhere nice. Give them a break.
- **Pray.** Let them know you are praying for them as well, not just for the sufferer.

Love responds from the heart, not just the head

No matter how thorough, logical and biblically literate a 'head' explanation of suffering is, when someone is actually suffering it may not help a bit. In fact, it may be hurtful and provoke anger. The love passage of 1 Corinthians 13 is that it makes it clear that words of knowledge and wisdom are no match for the genuine expression of love.

> *If I speak in the tongues of men or of angels, but do not have love, I am only a resounding gong or a clanging cymbal.*
> *1 Corinthians 13:1*

> *Suffering is only intolerable when nobody cares. One continually sees that faith in God and his care is made infinitely easier by faith in someone who has shown kindness and sympathy.*
> *Cicely Saunders[26]*

The great Christian author C. S. Lewis experienced a 'head to heart' transition. When he wrote his book *The Problem of Pain* in 1940, it was a deeply intellectual book. Then in 1960 his wife died and his understanding went from his head more to his heart.

> *No one ever told me that grief felt so like fear... We were promised sufferings. They were part of the program. We were even told, 'Blessed are they that mourn,' and I accept it. I've got nothing that I hadn't bargained for. Of course it is different when the thing happens to oneself, not to others, and in reality, not imagination...*
>
> *Talk to me about the truth of religion and I'll listen gladly. Talk to me about the duty of religion and I'll listen submissively. But don't come talking to me about the consolations of religion or I shall suspect that you don't understand.*
> *C S Lewis*[27]

Responding from the heart and not just the head includes not trying to give theologised answers but *listening*. The biblical explanation of suffering is important at some stage, but only at the right time, and only if delivered in just the right way. Ultimately, the heart and the head have to be aligned to understand the Christian view of suffering. Focus only on the heart and you can end up depressed or angry, but focus only on the head and you can end up lacking empathy.

> **THE HEART AND THE HEAD HAVE TO BE IN SYNC WHEN IT COMES TO SUFFERING**

Supporting others in suffering is about seeking to respond like Jesus did, not just with intellectual answers but by being moved with compassion and reaching out in kindness to help. Not doing so has caused many sufferers deep grief and lasting bitterness at the hands of well-meaning people. But when friends and family respond heart-to-heart, there is an easing of suffering, a feeling that someone cares and a sense that you are not doing the tough journey alone.

I know it can be hard at times to find the energy to think about these things, but I encourage you to do so. If they are understood and enacted, those who suffer in any context, church or not, will feel deeply loved and cared for. In the process, those who care for them will grow in wisdom and compassion.

Key points

- Families, friends and church members can learn to respond to suffering in ways that are helpful.
- Jesus-style engagement is about
  - listening before speaking
  - compassion
  - following words with actions
  - responding regardless of status
  - fearlessness.
- 'LEAP' is a useful way to remember what to do—Listen, Empathise, Act, Pray.
- 'Caring for carers' is a beautiful thing that a church community can do.

PART 3

Some Specific Types of Suffering Experienced Today

Chapter 7

Cancer

I have cancer. Cancer doesn't have me.
Marco Calderon[28]

Cancer affects virtually all families, yet they often don't understand how to respond to the diagnosis, especially if it is terminal (as it often is). This chapter talks specifically about terminal cancer—the diagnosis, the journey and how to face the end well.

Everyone is afraid of cancer

People can receive many sorts of bad health news such as that they have debilitating motor neurone disease. But it is cancer that people generally worry about, mostly because it is common. Almost everyone can identify someone in their family or friendship circle that has had it.

Over nine million people die of cancer each year in the world, and millions of others receive the bad news that they have cancer but survive it. It can occur at any age. It is scary because it is seen as a disease of prolonged, progressively worsening suffering, both from the symptoms of the disease itself—pain, fatigue, breathlessness, body wasting and more—and from the side effects of treatment.

I have cared for thousands of patients with cancer. It has been a journey of discovery as I have watched them respond to the diagnosis, therapy and prospect of dying, and then watched their loved ones cope with the grief.

THE SIX MOST FATAL CANCERS

Lung - Colorectal - Breast
Prostate - Skin - Stomach

Christians fear terminal cancer too

Christians suffering from cancer mostly have an automatic 'family' of caring individuals who will bring food, talk with them and pray for them. But they often also have to balance their illness with the ongoing optimism generated by the faith and encouragement of Christian friends, especially the repeated generation of false hopes if and when their disease becomes progressive.

Knowing that each of us is special to God means that when something like cancer happens, it is easier to assume that this is not a surprise to him.

> And even the very hairs of your head are all numbered.
> So don't be afraid; you are worth more than many sparrows.
> Matthew 10:30-31

However, that also creates a challenge. Am I going to be healed, either miraculously or via an extraordinary response to treatment, or not? I have seen both. But it is obvious that most Christians with terminal cancer are not healed. Dealing with that reality creates extra layers of issues for Christians that most unbelievers do not have to negotiate.

Being afraid of cancer can make some believers think they are not loved by God. Sometimes they have a mistaken notion that God's love is supposed to drive out fear (1 John 4:18), forgetting that Jesus himself experienced fear at the prospect of suffering and death in the Garden of Gethsemane. From my experience, however, I would say that in general being a Christian makes the journey with cancer easier, though of course it is still tough.

You can die well or die badly

Although some people say they would rather 'just drop dead' or die in their sleep, in many ways I feel that cancer is probably a preferable way to go. It provides an opportunity to say goodbye, to get closure, to write or tell your story (including your faith journey) for your kids and grandkids, to tell family and friends how much they have meant to you, and to prepare them all for your death and their ongoing life after you have gone.

A senior Christian palliative care physician in our city told gathered medical students, 'When it is my turn to die, I am hoping that I die of cancer, not suddenly—I would look forward to that!'

> DYING SLOWLY OF CANCER PROVIDES AN
> OPPORTUNITY TO SAY GOODBYE, GET CLOSURE
> AND PASS ON YOUR BELIEFS

But some patients, including Christians, die badly, and sometimes medical staff, family, friends and others make that process worse, not better. In the end, you can take the news of cancer well or take it badly, you can do the journey well or do it badly, and you can die well or die badly. It depends on how it is handled.

Dying from cancer creates suffering for both the patient and their close family. And, to put it bluntly, when the patient dies, their suffering is over, but the suffering of the family carries on. If the patient does not die well, that suffering can create prolonged grief and lead to bitterness. This applies to believers and non-believers alike.

Beginning the journey

In chapter 4 I looked at how to respond to the bad news of impending suffering, and everything I said there is relevant here. Here are some further tips.

RECEIVING THE NEWS
Getting a diagnosis of cancer, particularly if it is incurable, is serious and understandably stressful. It is unquestionably one of the most unforgettable days of a person's life. Deeply poignant moments stay in the mind and impact us forever, so it is vitally important to understand how powerful that experience is, for good or bad.

Similarly, it is vital to realise that the way family and friends respond to the news will also have a big impact, for good or bad. You can help to make it easier for them to cope, or make it harder and even hurt them.

Shocking news sears its way into our memories forever

Don't receive the news alone. This is your decision, but I strongly recommend going to the consultation where you will receive test results with a 'significant other'. This may be your partner and/or an adult child, some other relative, or even a close friend or pastor.

Some patients, men in particular, imagine this is best done alone without their wife there, in case she gets emotional. I disagree—my experience is that men get just as emotional but don't show it, and women are often more practical in these situations.

Make sure you get clear information. When you or your family or community have received this, you will be better equipped to handle things. This is another reason to have someone with you: once you receive the news, you will be hit by an emotional tidal wave and your head will go into a spin, so having another person present makes it more likely that the correct information will be received and passed on to family and friends.

This information includes discussing the prognosis and next steps. As mentioned in chapter 4, sometimes the prognosis may be held back by a doctor if a patient does not wish to know (10% are like that).

Tell others—family, friends, pastor, home group members. This can be done in writing first so the details can be delivered accurately and associated social anxiety avoided (I discussed how to do this in chapter 4). Open communication that allows for sharing and support helps the journey enormously.

EARLY REACTIONS

When bad news about cancer is expected, people often feel a sense of resignation and even relief that at least they know what it is. Christians and non-believers respond about the same at this point. Other emotional reactions vary a lot, but knowing what can happen helps you to be prepared.

Bad news affects more than just the sufferer

Typical emotions experienced by cancer sufferers and their loved ones are:
- **shock** and disbelief, particularly if they are feeling and looking very well
- **fear** about the way things will turn out and the way they might die
- **sadness** at a sense of life wasted or unfinished (especially for parents)

- **regret** at the time spent working rather than with people they care about
- **grief** at the fact they will not see children grow up or will leave their partner alone
- **anxiety** about the impact of death on family (especially children), friends, work and ministry
- **anger** at health professionals, work, God, even themselves
- **guilt** about smoking, letting kids get sunburnt, etc.
- **avoidance**—not confronting the truth and lying to others

If such responses make a sufferer isolate themselves, they can create loneliness for those with cancer or their family. Another common emotion is anxiety about losing control, something very difficult for people who are normally in control of their lives. This can feel overwhelming.

Cancer sufferers and their loved ones will often have surging emotions, sometimes feeling quite normal and other times devastated by disbelief. Everyone deals with it in their own way, including every family.

EFFECTS ON FAMILIES AND FRIENDS

The diagnosis of cancer will impact everyone who cares about the sufferer. Although family and friends experience many of the same emotions that patients do, they have the added emotion of guilt when fear and grief happen. This comes from the possibility of losing their loved on, fear at how the illness will impact their lives, and guilt at feeling egocentric when they don't actually have the cancer.

If you are the one with cancer, you may be disappointed at family and friends who stay away and pleasantly surprised at those who step up when you don't expect it. Expect 'happy faces' to be put on, plus over-caring and avoidance in its various forms. Expect inappropriate words. Friends may deny the illness or play down any fears. However, supportive family and friends do make a big difference. Despite imperfections, churches are usually good at this.

Cancer impacts the whole family

Cancer has a major effect on marriages and reactions differ. Some face the challenges together, but for others it generates problems and opens up wounds and existing problems that need counselling.

When my husband Paul was just 49, he showed signs of a brain tumour. About three weeks after the operation I went on a trip to Italy with my daughter to attend a wedding. Paul would not let me stay home and wanted me to go despite his terminal diagnosis. It was when we sat on the plane as it took off that I started to cry, and my daughter did too. I was asking God, 'How can this happen to us?' I cried at the enormity of it all. I didn't want it to be true. It was so weird. I felt anger. The reality of it was dawning on me—I didn't want to be without Paul for the rest of my life. And when I was walking around in Rome, I looked at the old couples and I cried repeatedly knowing that Paul and I would not grow old together and would never attend future weddings together. I thought this is just not fair.
Judith Curtis

Perspectives for walking the journey

Again, this whole book is a guide that will help you on the long and difficult cancer journey. I have found three perspectives are helpful for doing the journey well.

Cancer doesn't have to own you. As scary and lethal as cancer can be, it is not who you are. You are a wonderfully made, special person who is unique in God's eyes and deeply loved. Think about that, as hard as it might be, so that cancer does not control your life. Cancer will invade your life, but you do not have to be held captive to it.

> Be strong and courageous. Do not be afraid or terrified because of them, for the Lord your God goes with you; he will never leave you nor forsake you.
> Deuteronomy 31:6

Avoid self-recrimination. It is natural to feel anxious about what lies ahead, especially if the cancer is terminal. Anxiety at this point is not sinful. Sometimes Christians feel guilty that they are anxious, thinking that if they were more faithful, more spiritual, they would be more at peace. After all, doesn't the Bible tell us that?

> Do not be anxious about anything, but in every situation, by prayer and petition, with thanksgiving, present your requests to God. And the peace of God, which transcends all understanding, will guard your hearts and your minds in Christ Jesus.
> Philippians 4:6–7

I don't think such self-recrimination is fair. Being confronted with the reality of serious illness and the prospect of death has many implications, especially for your spouse, family and friends. It is an act of kindness to feel for them and thus to be anxious.

Plan for the worst, hope for the best. I discussed this approach in chapter 4. For the Christian, hoping for the best means praying for healing and for a good response to therapy. I *do* believe that God can work miracles, and sometimes he does. I have seen it. However, despite the fact that you don't think the timing is very good, God might actually be saying, 'Well done, good and faithful servant. Your time on earth is coming to an end. You will be coming home to me.' Recognising this is a crucial step in managing your expectations.

The journey's end

Patients sometimes ask me, 'How will I die? What will the end look like?' I love that question because it shows they have a healthy view of dying and are pretty much ready for it.

As already stated, you can die well or die badly. Here are some thoughts about dying well.

Embrace palliative care. I love palliative care. Virtually all of the nurses and doctors in this field that I have engaged with have been wonderful, professional and caring. I have no hesitation in referring my patients to palliative care, including Christians. For believers, palliative care some-times feels like an admission of failure. It is not. High quality palliative care services help people die well.

Ask medical staff direct questions and make it clear you want honest answers. I find that my patients are afraid to ask questions if the answers might be frightening (involving pain, breathlessness or nausea, for example). So I tend to jump in and give them answers to the unknowns. However, towards the end, I recommend that whatever you are worried about, don't be afraid to ask the medical staff direct questions. They may not know what is going on in your head and heart, and therefore may not know what to say pre-emptively.

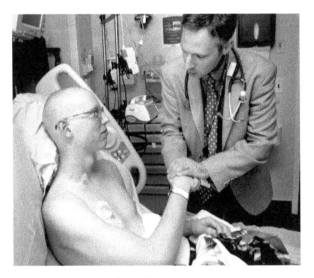

Insist on honest answers

Be honest with your family. When I lived in London, I remember the vicar of my church telling the congregation about visiting a parishioner who was dying in hospital. On the way in, the family pulled him aside and said, 'Michael, he's dying in there, but whatever you do, don't let on that you know because the news would kill him.' He then went in and began talking to his parishioner, who signalled to him to come close and whispered, 'Michael, I'm dying and I am okay with it, but whatever you do, don't let my family know that you know because the news would kill them.' I don't know what Michael did about it, but I'm sure he would have tried to get them together talking honestly, holding hands, saying goodbye and weeping, and maybe even laughing together.

It can be agonising to have those vital, honest conversations

It is vitally important to be honest with your family towards the end. Lies and avoidance do not help anyone. I acknowledge that it can be agonising to have those vital, honest conversations with people you love. But to not do so makes it harder, not easier.

Don't avoid actually saying goodbye. There is a deep poignancy about saying goodbye. A close friend of mine in the USA was dying of cancer. I called in to see him whenever I was in the country, and we would sit around talking over a glass of wine. Finally he realised he had only a few weeks to live, so we skyped and at the end said goodbye. I said, 'I love you, mate. Thanks for being such a good friend.' He did the same.

I know that his wife overheard us talking and was crying in the background, but she really appreciated the honesty and warmth of that goodbye conversation. I am glad not to be left wishing I had said something but didn't. Jesus had no problem saying goodbye to his disciples.

Celebrate your life. It's easy to get locked into the terminal stage of suffering until you and your family imagine that it is the defining moment of life. It is not. So when it gets to the end, talk about all the good things of your life, the good times with people, the things you've learnt. Laugh about your mistakes and celebrate your life. Complete memoirs. Let the family understand how grateful you are for the celebratory, wonderful things in life. That will make it easier for them and less morose for you.

Don't avoid saying goodbye

Be future looking. I sometimes remind my children that I will die one day, not to make them grieve in anticipation, but to encourage us all to seize the day and celebrate it.

I also want them to know what I think about dying. To me it's like cricket. Sometimes a batter boringly blocks the ball defensively all day long. In contrast, I have played adventurous shots throughout my innings. But you never know when you're going get the unplayable delivery that will get you out. When that happens, I will head back to the pavilion with my bat under my arm, removing my batting gloves and saying to the new batter coming in, 'Hey, I've had a great innings! Now it's your turn.'

I also tell them that although they will cry when I'm gone, I would rather they didn't give in to sadness and wishing I was still there. I would prefer them to think of the good things I taught them and pay them forward to their children and other people in their lives. Jesus did that too. Then I will 'live on' here on earth.

Terminal cancer is scary. You want it to go away. God definitely sometimes heals people supernaturally, and we should ask for that, but it does not typically happen. So we are left to decide whether we will die badly or well, because it is largely up to us. Dying well leaves those left behind in a better state than does dying badly, because grief handled well does make people better rather than bitter—I have seen that many times.

Key points

- Christians are frightened of terminal cancer too.
- Some believers die well and some die badly despite their faith.
- Cancer doesn't have to own you.
- God may heal you, or he may say, 'Well done, good and faithful servant. It's time to come home.'
- Tell friends and family honestly about the diagnosis.
- Plan for the worst, hope for the best.
- As the end approaches, celebrate life.

CHAPTER 8

Chronic illness
and pain

*Behind every chronic illness is just a person trying to find
their way in the world. We want to find love and be loved
and be happy just like you. We want to be successful and do
something that matters. We're just dealing with unwanted
limitations in our hero's journey.*
Glenn Schweitzer[29]

The purpose of this chapter is to highlight the
commonness of chronic illness, its effects and
the fact that it is usually hidden from others,
especially in a church community.

I suffered an horrendous backyard accident one day which made me deeply aware of the effects of excruciating chronic pain. In the late afternoon of a warm Sunday, a circular saw kicked backwards out of some timber and ripped through my left leg, bounced off the bone and then ripped through my right leg. The huge, gaping wounds spurted blood and made me think I would die.

When I got to the Emergency Department, a doctor attempted twice to clip the artery but succeeded only in crushing a major nerve. This felt like multiple high-voltage electric shock waves surging through my entire body, and I screamed in agony. After a long operation I realised that the cut nerve would now be a physical disability, and as a sportsman I was over-whelmed by a powerful sense of loss. I found myself sobbing helplessly.

A near-fatal mistake—a circular saw ripped through both my legs

But then worse torture hit me. After two weeks in hospital, I returned home in increasing pain from causalgia, a feeling of burning hot pokers being pushed into the bottom of my left foot. The next day, as if things weren't bad enough, my mother's family doctor rang to inform me that he had just diagnosed terminal cancer in her. I put the phone down and wept and wept.

The 'burning hot coals' pain became more severe and insistent. This is the sort of pain that soldiers experience when a land mine blows a leg off, driving them to alcohol, drugs or suicide. I was unable to focus and concentrate, and I developed analgesic toxicity from taking too many painkillers. I lost 12 kilograms in weight. It went on for months, and the level of severe pain did not respond to any therapy. My physicians started planning more and more radical approaches, but I was too distracted to focus or care.

Chronic versus acute suffering

Chronic suffering is different from acute suffering. If you develop appendicitis or get an abscess you can reasonably expect to be back to your normal self soon. But that is not true for conditions like chronic pain, physical disability or unrelenting or recurring illness. Without immediate hope of a return to normal life, anxiety, depression and fear of the future take over. Chronic illness can end up ruling a person's life.

Patients with acute conditions can adjust quickly to their diseases, but the suffering of chronic illness never goes away. We plead with God. Friends pray for us. Hope is eventually lost, and when that happens, suffering increases and faith shrinks. If there is no obvious precipitating event, some people who suffer with chronic illness feel like frauds and apologise to doctors or pastors for 'wasting their time'. They would feel more justified if they were dying of cancer.

Everyone with chronic suffering faces challenges to their very person-hood. Behind the often false smiles is a person who is required, every day, to get up and face extra physical and emotional difficulties over and above the struggles that life deals to everyone. This can be exhausting and isolating.

The reality of chronic suffering

Chronic conditions are becoming more common. We are living longer, and those who might previously have died from the condition they are suffering from may now live longer and pay the physical and emotional costs of long-term symptoms and health care. The World Health Organization describes chronic illnesses as 'a hidden epidemic'.

The sorts of chronic conditions that generate suffering include neuro-muscular diseases (ranging from fibromyalgia to multiple sclerosis), visual problems, chronic lung disease, diabetes, chronic hepatitis, chronic heart failure, ulcerative colitis, chronic kidney disease, morbid obesity and Parkinson's disease. There are many more. In Australia, the overall cost to the health care system of some of these chronic conditions is around $6 billion per year while lost productivity is estimated to cost approximately $13 billion per year. The Centre for Disease Control puts this figure at $147 billion per year in the United States, and it is proportionately similar in other Western countries.

EXAMPLES OF CHRONIC SUFFERING

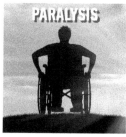
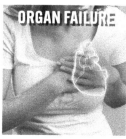
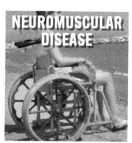
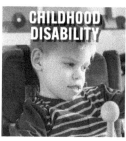

Chronic illnesses like these lead to major lifestyle changes:
- social isolation, including from church and home groups
- cessation of enjoyable activities
- obsession with the illness and its therapy
- morose, negative thought patterns
- apathy
- erosion of faith and loss of hope
- evolving anger leading to internment in a 'prison of bitterness'

By isolating themselves, chronic sufferers cut themselves off from those who are likely to be the most supportive groups in their family, work and community circles. This can lead to depression and anxiety, with lack of energy, sleep difficulties and the side effects of painkiller drugs. Christians can feel guilty at this stage—why am I not embracing God's promises?

Relationships can also be affected in varying ways, adding to the emotional challenges. Some people will 'blame' the sufferer for lack of recovery. This can also work the opposite way—a family member can take excessive personal responsibility, including by praying obsessively for the sufferer's recovery and calling on others to do the same, then feeling like a failure if no improvement occurs. Sufferers can also feel like they are letting others down.

> *Chronic physical pain can be debilitating, not only to the body but to the mind and heart as well. I struggle multiple times a week feeling as though my husband and my children deserve better. I feel like I let God down because I cannot be the helpmate and mother* he *wants me to be.*
> Diane Ferreira[30]

The suffering of chronic pain

Prolonged, debilitating pain is a special cause of chronic suffering. Whether from an accident like mine or from headaches, severe arthritis, cancer, back pain, neuralgias or some other condition—or from no obvious cause at all—it can disable sufferers for long periods and render them unable to work or care for their family.

Chronic pain that is not linked to an event can be hard to understand, so many sufferers are reluctant to describe their pain. They become discouraged by the failure of treatments and the flagging compassion of carers, including in churches. Both patients and professional staff can dismiss the emotional challenges associated with chronic pain as they strive to find solutions. Pain can attack your very sense of who you are as a person.

> *I stepped off the tracks of 'normal, everyday life' into the no-man's land of chronic pain, then depression... After some months of unsuccessful treatment and fed by my own fears and anxieties, the pain gradually expanded into a black hole of existential despair that sucked away my hope and zest for life... Anyone who has been in the throes of unrelenting physical pain knows the hard truth: Pain eats away at your personhood.*
> **Liuan Huska**[31]

It is impossible to escape severe chronic pain. When you think about it, all of us are born in pain (Genesis 2), we may die in pain and we certainly experience pain regularly throughout our lives. At its deepest level, pain is important in human survival—from a speck of dust in an eye to pain in the feet when we walk on a hot road, pain keeps us from damage. But prolonged physical and emotional pain can take over our mental focus in an unwanted and unwelcome way, continually drawing us into the present moment with the alarm signals ringing, giving us no option but to try to escape. And when escape is impossible, it is no wonder that depression, frustration and anxiety result.

The suffering caused by pain flows not just from the pain itself but from our response to it. We have a massive array of medical interventions today to reduce pain, so this generation expects to be pain-free. Pain that we did not ask for, that ambushes us and doesn't go away, is the most debilitating and causes the most suffering. Guilt can follow.

> *I want to serve, be involved at church, and become immersed in Christian community, but so often I can't do these things because of my pain.*
> *Esther Smith*[32]

Hope as a cost and a gift

After my accident I lost hope. I was in a daze. Loss of hope is a scary thing. Depression may be next.

For those enduring chronic suffering, holding on to hope can be costly. But even here the promises of God we saw in chapter 3 hold true: you are ultimately indestructible, God understands your suffering, Jesus is with you in what you're going through and you can grow and bloom from your pain.

> *This is my comfort in my affliction, that your promise gives me life.*
> *Psalm 119:50*

You are not your suffering. If you suffer chronic illness or severe pain, you risk becoming so identified with that type of suffering that it can become your identity. You are no longer the person you were but have become a victim. The pain becomes who you are. But this is not the truth. It is better to see the pain as something that you, as a unique and special creation, are enduring.

> *Sometimes I wonder when the pain and restrictions will go away, but inevitably I find myself beat down once again believing that this will never leave me. That this illness is who I am both now and forever. But then there are times where I recognize that this is not my identity, I remember who God has called me to be. He has not labeled me 'broken,' 'inadequate,' or 'mistake.' He has called me 'daughter (1 John 3:1),' 'holy (Colossians 1:22),' 'righteous (Romans 3:20),' and 'redeemed (Psalm 107:2).' This illness is not me. It may be part of my story, but it will never be strong enough to define me.*
> *Hannah Bowers[33]*

Chronic suffering can be a gift. It is hard sometimes to appreciate this. The famous Christian physician Paul Brand wisely called chronic pain 'the gift nobody wants'. But just as there is hope for any Christian who experiences acute suffering, those who experience chronic suffering likewise can find that spiritual benefits flow.

Some examples of how chronic suffering has enriched life include:

- Intimacy with God, as Job experienced.

> *My ears had heard of you but now my eyes have seen you.*
> *Job 42:5*

- Better insights into suffering.

> *If you had never known physical pain in your life, how could you appreciate the nail scarred hands with which Jesus Christ will meet you?*
> *Joni Eareckson Tada[34]*

- A new capacity to help others.

> *Praise be to the God and Father of our Lord Jesus Christ, the Father of compassion and the God of all comfort, who comforts us in all our troubles, so that we can comfort those in any trouble with the comfort we ourselves receive from God.*
> *2 Corinthians 1:3–4*

- Increased insight to give to others.

> *As I've simply shared my struggle with chronic pain from the pulpit, I am discovering dozens of fellow members facing*

similar pains—most of which are more severe than mine. I'm realizing my journey with pain has enabled me to offer God's healing presence in a more personally connected way.
Jeremy Linneman[35]

The hope of the resurrection. One obvious piece of hope that is offered to Christians is that of a new body in the next life. I did not think much about that when I was young, but I have since met many Christians who suffer from chronic illnesses or pain for whom this is a major source of hope. What a beautiful thing it is to be able to say, 'He will wipe every tear from their eyes' (Rev. 21:4).

> *So we do not lose heart. Though our outer self is wasting away, our inner self is being renewed day by day.*
> *2 Corinthians 4:16 (ESV)*

> *I consider that our present sufferings are not worth comparing with the glory that will be revealed in us.*
> *Romans 8:18*

WHAT CAME FROM
MY PERSONAL CHRONIC PAIN

After my terrible circular saw injury, I experienced months of excruciating, debilitating pain. Then one night I attended my church home group meeting. I didn't want to go, but my wife encouraged me to mix with friends. They laid hands on me and prayed for me, but to be honest, although I was grateful for their care and attention, I was distracted by the pain, didn't feel much faith and didn't expect anything to come of it So I was honestly surprised when that searing pain miraculously almost disappeared over the next two days. It does still come back to bite me from time to time, and I still have hypersensitivity of the left foot so that if I tread on anything barefoot, I feel severe pain—I see that as a reminder of God's strategy for us, like Paul's affliction was for him.

This whole experience changed my life. In an undefinable way I feel it 'softened me up', and others have mentioned this also. It taught me that anyone, no matter how generally competent and emotionally strong, can in certain circumstances become vulnerable and distressed and have difficulty coping. I am now much more sympathetic to others who have chronic pain. And I understand why traumatic accidents can produce psychological problems if not dealt with adequately—I still have trouble talking about the incident to others and when I do I sometimes get a rapid heart and start sweating. I always cry.

This awful journey taught me many important lessons. First, I learned that I needed to listen better and understand people's pain, because it can be hard for many to express just how bad pain is and how much it is eating away at them. Second, I had a deep experience of the love of God, including an amazing feeling while being treated in the Emergency Department of his love holding me up when I felt like I would sink. Knowing that love in an experiential way is one of the things that makes me weep whenever I sing about the love of God in church. Third, the experience has helped me realise that the wonderful promise that we are ultimately indestructible, despite huge suffering, is true.

How the church can respond to those with chronic suffering

Churches are a great potential source of support for sufferers, but we do better when a problem is acute, such as an accident or sudden illness. Like the rest of the community, with chronic suffering we tend to get compassion fatigue—many stop helping and start avoiding.

As church communities we can learn compassionate words and body language that don't require a huge time commitment. Creating specific support groups is another approach. Importantly, even if friends and members of the church community cannot commit to long-term support, they can commit to learning how to respond to someone with chronic suffering.

> *Too often, when I've mentioned my chronic pain to fellow believers, they've responded with a possible cure or treatment. 'You should see a chiropractor.' 'How much magnesium are you getting?' 'Are you familiar with essential oils?' Certainly these responses mean well, but they aren't the most loving. Instead, we can offer each other a listening ear, offer sincere encouragement, and pray for the sufferer.*
> *Jeremy Linneman[36]*

Because a lot of chronic suffering is hidden, it can be hard for sufferers to communicate their problems and receive help. Here are some tips for supporting them over and above those listed in other chapters.

THINGS TO DO

Follow the LEAP steps (chapter 6):

- **Listen.** Chronic sufferers are aware that people get tired of their story. Let them tell it.
- **Empathise.** They might become reluctant to say exactly how they feel. Empathy can give them permission to tell the truth. Weep with them, or just sit with them.
- **Act.** Help them do something they haven't been able to do for a while—visit the beach or a park, go fishing, attend a sporting event or concert. Don't just say, 'If there is anything I can do …'
- **Pray.** Tell them you are praying for them.

THINGS TO AVOID

- Unhelpful words (simple solutions or 'snap out of it' responses)
- 'Biblical' explanations and clichés ('God has a reason for this', 'God is teaching you patience', etc.)
- Dismissal ('I'm sure it will go away', 'You don't need to worry.')
- Trivialisation (comparing the chronic sufferer to someone 'worse off'; 'You're exaggerating—you look just fine', 'It's all in your mind.')
- Saying 'I understand'—you can't and won't
- The urge to 'explain' chronic suffering
- Praying instead of visiting. It is easy to avoid those with chronic problems. Be aware that compassion fatigue is common, so don't go missing in action.
- Outstaying your welcome—pain is tiring

It is hard to get this right. In fact you will get it wrong many times, as I have. Please don't over criticise yourself. Forgive yourself and try again. One of the great joys in life is to become pretty comfortable and skilled at caring for those who are suffering so that you enjoy the experience rather than shying away from it.

Key points

- Chronic illness is a 'hidden epidemic'.
- Behind every chronic illness is just a person trying to find their own way in the world.
- Pain is a special cause of chronic suffering, often hidden and impossible to escape.
- Chronic illness and pain can cause social isolation, including from church and home groups.
- Chronic suffering can erode faith and hope, but it can also be a launch pad for deep Christian growth.
- There are many things for church friends to say and do that help (and many to avoid).

CHAPTER 9

Mental illness

*As a Christian, depression tempted me to distrust God. I was
desperately seeking deliverance He seemed to withhold from
me. 'Why won't you lift me out of this pit?' I'd cry. 'Aren't
you a deliverer? Why do the voices of despair sound so much
louder than yours?'*
Mary Keith[37]

> The purpose of this chapter is to help readers
> better understand the nature of mental
> illness and its profound effects on the life and
> spirituality of sufferers and those around them.

No book on suffering can ignore the pain caused by mental illness. Such illnesses include depression, anxiety disorders (prolonged fear not based on actual threat), bipolar disorder, schizophrenia (mixed-up thoughts, delusions or hallucinations), personality disorders and eating disorders such as anorexia and bulimia. People who suffer these problems, especially Christians, often blame themselves for not being able to bounce back from them.

It is fair to say that the church has not dealt very well with mental illness over the years—or rather, has not known *how* to deal with it—though things are changing now.

Mental illness has a major impact not only on the sufferer but on family and friends. Yet it is often trivialised, or solutions are simplified by those who do not understand. The sufferer can feel they are wasting everyone's time, and ultimately, that they are a waste of space themselves.

MY FATHER'S DECLINE INTO DEPRESSION

During my teenage years I saw the suffering of mental illness and its effects up close. The personal story of my father's painful, deep depression is just one of millions of similar stories.

In our younger years Dad was happy. He was a good man who believed that success in life was measured by what you put into it, not what you got out of it. He worked in a local factory as a clerk and was a very active community member, well regarded as the Deputy Mayor and president of a number of local community groups.

He was also a good dad, taking us camping and early-morning swimming down the river, and happy to talk with my brother and me openly about life. Some of my friends had aloof dads and told me that they wished their dads were more like mine.

But then Dad fell into a full-blown mid-life crisis—a combination of loss of youth, personal illness, death of parents, evolving independence of adolescent kids and spouse, and a sense of disappointment about work and lack of achievement. He experienced all this within a few years. Poor Dad copped a 'perfect storm', but he didn't understand what hit him.

Like so many young men, Dad had 'learnt' to drink and smoke while serving during the Second World War. But he was unable to stop, especially when under pressure. From alcoholism he lurched into depression—drunk at night then depressed for days.

This went on for three years. It was hard for me to watch my hero degrading himself. I recall being woken one night by the sound of him crawling along the passageway, so drunk he couldn't even walk. I heard him scratching at the door to his bedroom for 10 minutes, trying to find the handle.

Like all families of those with depression, we suffered too. Mum struggled a lot during this time. She used to cook his dinner but leave it in the warmer of the wood stove, never knowing if and when he would come home. My brother and I also suffered. Dad was never physically violent, but he brought a black cloud of anger whenever he arrived home. He had previously brought humour and fun, but now he brought ill temper.

Our family car was quiet but had a gear stick that rattled loudly when the engine was turned off. Whenever we heard that rattle outside—'the danger rattle'—we knew Dad was back. We would all jump up from our chairs and, like cockroaches when you open a drawer, try to scuttle off to our rooms to hide from his words of anger and accusation.

Christians are not immune

The suffering of mental illness can be triggered by many different life events. It might be the death of a significant loved one such as a parent or a spouse; rapid changes in economic, educational or social status (including divorce or unemployment); conflict with others, including fellow church members; abuse or trauma; alcohol or drugs (though these may be used to cope rather than being the cause). Psychological distress induced by events like these is normal, but not everyone is tipped into a mental illness. Most individuals who go through these experiences regain control after the difficult period, but those with mental illness feel powerless to regain that control.

Mental illness causes suffering through feelings of distress, a reduced ability to function, changes in thinking, alternations of mood, loneliness and unrelenting sadness. Another problem arises when those around the person get worn out from caring, become easily irritated and impatient, and start avoiding them, leaving them isolated.

Most mental illnesses can be treated effectively by medical professionals and community-based services. Some people require hospitalisation to stabilise symptoms, but this is not usual. Unfortunately, because of the stigma of mental illness, many people, particularly Christians, avoid or delay treatment.

Christians are not immune from these disorders, and although they are more likely to have a supportive community around them, they can face extra challenges, both in their own thinking and from their church. Believers suffering from mental illness often feel like failures because they should be living the 'abundant life': 'Why doesn't God just lift me out of the mire when I cry out to him? He seems to have left me there—so it must be my fault.' Thus it can become even harder to call the doctor or a local crisis line. It is possible too that they feel judged by their Christian community, whether they are actually being judged or not.

> *I waited patiently for the LORD; he turned to me and heard my cry. He lifted me out of the slimy pit, out of the mud and mire; he set my feet on a rock and gave me a firm place to stand. He put a new song in my mouth, a hymn of praise to our God.*
> *Psalm 40:1–3*

Depression: the cloud that never lifts

It is not possible to discuss every mental illness in this book, but there is one that is common and often misunderstood both in church communities and by individuals: depression. Depression is a good example of the issue of mental suffering.

Depression is one of the most common mental disorders. In 2017–18, 10.4% of Australian adults experienced depression or feelings of depression. That represents over 1 in 10 adults—in a church of 400 people it means around 40 will struggle with some kind of depressive feelings. Do you know who they are? Probably not. I don't know them all in our church either. It might surprise you to know they may well be the busy, efficient, effective high-achieving leaders who look happy and contented, not the lazy pessimists.

Depression has been described as 'a cloud that never lifts, but that follows you around pouring rain on you when everyone else is standing in the sunshine. Nothingness. No hope, no joy, no desire, no goodness, no values, no interest.' It induces 'a spiritual or emotional fog that stubbornly clouds out hope and happiness.' 'No other disease, physical or mental, reinforces and feeds itself as depression does.' Sufferers put on a happy face, but inside they are weeping.

Depression hurts not only the sufferer but also those closest to them. Irritability sets off family conflicts. Negative thought patterns become a prism of pessimism for everyone. Withdrawal of the sufferer from others, or others from the sufferer, generates feelings of rejection. Partners feel stressed and overwhelmed with the continual concern of watching out for suicide. The result is burnout, exhaustion and risk of partner depression ('depression is contagious').

Families can be major sources of comfort and even cure, but sometimes family members struggle to cope with the idea of depression in a loved one and deny its existence in various ways. Many people consider depression to be a manifestation of weakness, so they expect the sufferer to pull themselves together and snap out of it. Others go to the other extreme and try to fix it, submerging themselves in the fight. Both create problems and cause the depressed loved one to feel pressured to recover quickly.

Depression and the church

Depression is sometimes a touchy subject in Christian circles. Perspectives on mental disorders vary a lot throughout the church (though incorrect understanding of mental illness is also common in secular society). This means that sufferers often hide their problems or that their suffering is far worse than they let on. They wish someone would reach out and understand, but they are frightened of that too.

Christians often get confused about depression. They misread Bible verses such as 'the joy of the Lord is your strength' (Neh. 8:10) to mean that lack of joy is unspiritual. Other things that well-meaning Christians commonly get wrong about depression include that it is:

- a character defect or choice
- a spiritual disorder, sin or failure to show the fruit of the Spirit
- easily admitted to
- easily solved by quoting Bible verses (this can make things worse)
- always obvious (many hide it well, especially in a church, and even from doctors)
- uncommon
- often preached on.

The girl in the corner
She wants somebody to listen,
someone to understand.
But when she opens up,
Nobody wants to lend a hand.
Kaylee Everhaert[38]

The truth is that depression of some kind affects the lives of many Christians. It is not a stigma to be shunned, a failure of spirituality or faith, or a demonic attack. It is also not a church failure but an opportunity for the church to celebrate its Jesus-like empathy.

> *I had to realize that Christians can get depressed—and this is OK. Depression does not mean you have a weak relationship with God or that your faith isn't as strong as it should be. This was a revelation for me...*
>
> *I never expected to become depressed. I thought being a Christian, relying on faith, would garner me immunity from ever having that experience. I felt like church taught me to stay positive, never confessing or acknowledging the negative.*
> *LaKeisha Fleming*[39]

Telling a depressed person 'show more faith' or 'you must have hidden sin' is cruel. Asking someone to 'try' not being depressed is tantamount to asking someone who has had their hand cut off to stop bleeding. Faith in God's healing capability is important, but medical or psychiatric treatments are available, and to deny these to someone suffering from depression or other mental illnesses is harmful, risky and hurtful. People may drop out of church or home group because they can't face it due to their depression, not vice versa.

Clinical intervention

Often depression requires clinical intervention. The church is sometimes afraid of psychology, thinking that it is 'unspiritual'. But God gave us drugs and researchers. Just as we use well-researched drugs like antibiotics to treat pneumonia, so we need to be open to using well-researched anti-depressants when recommended.

Some Christians prefer to be treated by Christian psychologists or psychiatrists because they understand the full colour of their lives. Others prefer not to be—they worry that Christian presuppositions might override the flow of conversation and make them less free to disclose their inner feelings for fear of being judged. Individuals decide for themselves and often try different therapists until they find one that suits them.

> *As one who struggles with depression in spite of genuine faith, I have come to see the silver lining in it and am able to thank God for it... I know that God has a purpose even for my depression and that the end result will be good. This is not to say that one shouldn't fight depression, that it isn't difficult, and that there is no help for it. It is to say that it can be accepted, though painful, as coming from the hand of God for a purpose as he sees fit.*
>
> *Paul Toews[40]*

Suicide

Every day in Australia, around nine people commit suicide and 178 more *attempt* suicide. That's one person trying to kill themselves every eight minutes. Suicide is the leading cause of death among Australians aged 15 to 44. Three-quarters of those who take their own lives are men.

Suicide can be considered a complication of depression in the same way that heart failure can be a complication of a heart attack or paralysis a complication of a stroke. I described above my father's descent into deep depression and its effect on our family. I will now tell you how it got so bad that he tried to end his life.

> 'Suicide does not get rid of your problem, it just passes it on to those left behind.'

MY FATHER'S SUICIDE ATTEMPTS

Two months after his own father, also a chain smoker, dropped dead, Dad was admitted to hospital again. It wasn't for another heart attack (he had already had two despite being only 43 years old) but for injuries sustained in a drunken car accident. The hospital team found he was profoundly depressed. He confessed he had driven to a remote spot in the hills to kill himself but had phoned the Good Samaritans helpline and they helped him change his mind. The accident occurred while driving back home.

He didn't get any help for his depression, and over the next few months, when the alcohol no longer took away his pain, he decided the time had come to end it properly.

One night he came into my bedroom at 4.30 am, obviously drunk again, and woke me. He told me that he had taken a bottle of sleeping tablets. 'You'll need to look after Mum and the family,' he said. 'You're the oldest son, so it will be your responsibility.'

He walked out. The room was dark and my heart was racing. I tried to stay cool. My dad was about to die. But he was so utterly miserable, maybe he was right. Let him go, I thought—it would be better for everyone. I lay there weighing this up for five minutes (or so I thought; it was probably actually 30 seconds).

My heart still racing, I got up and walked to the kitchen. He was lying on the floor in his dressing gown, already asleep. The pills were working fast. The father I loved yet avoided, my hero growing up, was dying. I called an ambulance and went with him to the hospital.

THE CHURCH AND SUICIDE

Suicide has long been a contentious issue in the church. It has been considered a 'mortal sin', a moral and spiritual wrong, because it is contrary to nature (the preservation of life) and because God alone should decide when a person dies. Many still hold that view, often without ever thinking it through. But many within the church are forced to think it through, deeply, because Christians do take their own lives. That leaves family and fellow believers devastated, whether they were half expecting it to happen or not.

Even pastors commit suicide. Bill Lenz was the founder of Christ the Rock Community Church in Harrison, Wisconsin. Known for his authenticity and empathetic acceptance of people, he helped hundreds with their personal struggles. Yet he died by suicide after struggling for months with depression.

> *Bill was very open about things that he was going through. That's what made this so maddening and so confusing because he either didn't or couldn't share some of the deepness of what he was wrestling with.*
> **Curt Drexler**[41]

Similarly, Andrew Stoecklein was the lead pastor of Inland Hills Church in Chino, California. He was married and had three children. He took his own life when he was just thirty years old.

> *Last night, the love of my life, the father of my children and the pastor of our incredible church took his last breath and went to be with Jesus. It wasn't the miracle I was hoping for, but he is now in heaven with his dad, free of pain, free of depression and free of anxiety.*
> **Kayla Stoecklein**[42]

One reason Christians get surprised by suicide is that in many cases our faith prevents us from declining into suicidal situations. It provides meaning, purpose and knowledge that we can grow through our suffering, plus a community of loving carers and encouragement to be open about how we are doing in life. But wonderful as all that is, sometimes it is not enough.

Here are some truths about Christians who commit suicide. They are not bad people. They are not faithless or lacking in courage or strength. They are just struggling with sadness, shame, grief and hopelessness.

They are not heartless—indeed, they often take their own life to 'spare the family more pain' or because 'they will be better off without me'. In their distorted thinking, suicide can actually be an act of kindness, not selfishness.

Among the falsehoods Christians believe about suicide is the notion that a genuine Christian would never commit suicide, so their faith can't have been genuine—and even if it was, by committing suicide they have lost their salvation. Suicide is seen as the 'unforgivable sin' (Matt 12:32; Mk 3:28–29). But this is not so—the unforgivable sin is continual rejection of the Holy Spirit. Christians who take their own lives do not go to hell.

Sometimes people point out that the Bible describes no instance of a believer committing suicide, but this 'argument from silence' is not valid. Scripture does not cover every issue in life, but it would most likely have mentioned such cases if this was a critical spiritual issue above others.

THE RESPONSE OF FAMILY, FRIENDS AND CHURCH MEMBERS TO A SUICIDE

The grief that follows suicide is called 'complicated grief'. This is because grief at losing a loved one is complicated by trauma, guilt (including survivor's guilt) and shame. Guilt is typical: 'Why didn't I see this coming?' 'Why didn't I prevent it?' 'Is there something wrong with our church or our family?' 'Have I been too self-absorbed?' 'Maybe I should have spent more time with them ...'

A good friend of mine from football-playing days took his life 30 years after we stopped playing football together. I had caught up with him just the week before. I was devastated. For months I asked myself if there was anything else I could have said to him. Being a doctor and knowing that everyone does this didn't stop me feeling that guilt.

Billy Graham was once asked, by parents of a son who took his life after a struggle with drugs, alcohol and depression, whether God would forgive them or not. They were wracked with guilt. What did they do wrong and why were they such bad parents?

As with all suffering, some of the responses that Christians can have after a suicide are unhelpful. These include telling grieving loved ones things like 'God has a plan for this' or 'what doesn't kill you makes you stronger'. Sympathy for people's distress even leads some people to say 'how could God possibly do this to you?' or 'you should feel mad at him'.

When suicide happens in the family, don't cover up the truth from children. Lies don't work. Be careful, though, about timing and using the right words—perhaps something like, 'Daddy was very sick in his brain and he felt that he could not go on living. It is not anyone's fault. His sickness made him so confused that he felt that ending his life would make everyone better off. That's not his fault or anyone else's—it's what that sickness does to a person's brain. He actually really loved you, but he picked a bad way to show it. That's an example of how his brain was creating bad thoughts that he couldn't control.'

WHAT HAPPENED TO MY DAD?

Dad was in hospital for a long time and had counselling, medications and electroconvulsive therapy. He recovered brilliantly and was never majorly depressed again. Although he always remained a fairly heavy drinker, to my knowledge he only occasionally let himself go and got paralytic drunk.

I used to wonder why he came into my bedroom that night to wake me up. Now I know it was a cry for help—he wanted me to make a decision he couldn't make. I am glad I made it. Why me and not my mother? I understand this now too. Curiously, I feel kind of honoured by it.

Those years were tough, but I also treasure fond memories of Dad's life after that dark period. He rebounded, and he and mum became beautifully close again for the first time in decades. A few years after his suicide attempt, my brother and I attended the first ever Ashes cricket test in our city with him. The local town council recently named a community centre after him in a big, impressive ceremony to honour his years of service to the community.

I am proud of my dad. Not every profoundly depressed, suicidal person gets such a happy ending, but it is possible.

> While many are lost to their depression—helplessly wandering in their own darkness—Christians have somewhere to turn, truths to rehearse until our hearts catch up with the faith in our minds. Not only did Christ save and deliver the brokenhearted, but he experienced all the pains and temptations we face and more. At the cross, he dove headfirst into the darkness, so that we might have eternal, unfading, always-increasing hope and happiness.
> Marshall Segal[43]

Depression can go on for a long time. It can wear everyone out. If you are the one depressed, my heart reaches out to you. I acknowledge your pain and how overwhelming it can be. I also acknowledge how difficult it can be to speak about it to other Christians. I encourage you to find someone safe and share your feelings honestly.

Key points

- Psychological distress is normal and we can all get mental illness.
- Depression is not a character flaw, a choice, a stigma or a sin.
- Those around a depressed person, especially families, suffer too.
- Don't tell a depressed person 'show more faith' or 'you must have hidden sin'.
- Faith is important, but denying medical and psychological treatments is harmful, risky and hurtful—prayer is necessary but not always enough.
- Christians commit suicide too, including pastors. It is not a mortal sin.

CHAPTER 10

Conflict, anger and disappointment

No form of vice, not worldliness, not greed of gold, not drunkenness itself, does more to un-Christianize society than evil temper.
Henry Drummond[44]

> The purpose of this chapter is to discuss suffering in relationships. This can be deep, painful and all-consuming. Conflict, anger and disappointment can destroy peace. But if these are resolved well, relationships in families, marriages, workplaces, churches and neighbourhoods can be strengthened and deepened.

Conflict

> *There's been a quantum leap technologically in our age, but unless there's another quantum leap in human relations, unless we learn to live in a new way towards one another, there will be a catastrophe.*
> *Albert Einstein*[45]

Conflicts are an almost daily challenge in all families and workplaces. I recently asked a senior university leader and medical research institute director how much of his time he spends on 'people issues', particularly avoiding or managing conflicts. He surprised me when he said, 'Eighty per cent'. Stress in workplaces can cause people to stay away from work, with absenteeism costing national economies billions of dollars every year.

Conflicts are common everywhere

We would love to think that churches are different, but in addition to the usual causes of conflict we Christians have our own set of triggers: worship styles, length of services, songs, change, cross-cultural issues, who is in charge, what people say and a host of others. A Google search for the phrase "conflict in churches" today yielded 109,000 results.

It is wonderful that damaged people are attracted to churches, but we are a work in progress. Where two or more are gathered in Jesus' name, he is present (Matt 18:20)—and so is the potential for conflict. The Apostle Paul often had to deal with church conflicts. We are a family, and families always have issues to deal with.

Any conflict based on truth (a genuine issue) has a chance of being resolved (for example, if you have said or done something for which you need to apologise). But if conflict is based on error, it is ironically harder to resolve. And not all conflict *can* be resolved—it is important to understand that. Nonetheless, conflicts do in general provide an opportunity for healing and strengthening of relationships.

Some run from conflicts

The Gospels contain for me the two keys to preventing or dealing with conflict. Jesus was full of these two things: *grace* and **truth**.

> *We have seen his glory, the glory of the one and only Son,*
> *who came from the Father, full of grace and truth.*
> *John 1:14*

Grace and truth are embodied in two values that are part of many organisations' value statements: *respect* (grace) and *integrity* (truth). If organisations, including churches, could live by these two words alone, conflict would dramatically diminish or be quickly and respectfully resolved.

Grace in the Bible means a regard for another individual that they do not deserve. It is unconditional. That is God's attitude to us, and he asks us to have that attitude to others, giving them that same gift of undeserved love. Such grace has implications for us in our attitude to conflict, including in following Jesus' instruction to be intentional in loving enemies rather than seeking to win a fight or get revenge (Matt 5:38–45; cf. Lev 19:18; Rom 12:17–18). Grace should determine our style of approach to conflicts.

> *Let your conversation be always full of grace, seasoned with*
> *salt, so that you may know how to answer everyone.*
> *Colossians 4:6*

Truth is a fundamental characteristic of the love that God demands of us when engaging with others. Love 'rejoices with the truth' (1 Cor 13:6). Truth demands that we are interested in what is true rather than what is guesswork, gossip or lies. It also demands that we be interested in what is so rather than what we *want* to be so.

What might this look like in practice? Grace demands that *we see the person before the problem*. It means that our feelings, no matter how strong, are not more important than theirs. Truth demands that *we seek clarification rather than delivering an accusation*. It means that our opinion is not more important than what is true. Using these two rules will avoid or manage most conflicts.

> *Hot tempers cause arguments, but patience brings peace.*
> *Proverbs 15:18 (GNT)*

> *Never pay back evil for evil to anyone. Respect what is right in the sight of all people. If possible, so far as it depends on you, be at peace with all people.*
> *Romans 12:17–18 (NASB)*

> *Do not be overcome by evil, but overcome evil with good.*
> *Romans 12:21*

Although the desired outcome is peace and goodwill, however, we live in a fallen world and that doesn't always happen. Sometimes, despite using the best possible grace and truth processes, somebody will continue to be negative towards you, cold shoulder you and even accuse you of doing or saying things that are not true. If grace and truth don't bring change, self-care becomes critical.

SELF-CARE DURING CONFLICTS

- Don't rely on others changing. Even when exposed to the truth, some individuals refuse to change their views or their behaviour. Free yourself from their egocentricity. Don't make yourself vulnerable with them or be held captive by their lack of dignity and respect. Set firm boundaries.
- Meditate on the cross (see chapter 3). I have found this to be a wonderful tool.
- Respond in grace, doing good, but don't be 'gaslit' (that is, don't let the other person make you accept blame for their mistakes). Grace does not mean assuming you are wrong. See the facts, including the positive in yourself.

Anger

Anger is an emotion that can totally disrupt the function of our brains (our reasoning) and our lives. Many Christians have described to me what the level of suffering is like living with someone with anger issues. Unresolved anger can have a big impact on families, workplaces and church communities. But there are strategies that can fix it.

> *People with quick tempers cause a lot of quarreling and trouble.*
> Proverbs 29:22 (GNT)

Anger is an intense expression of emotion involving a hostile response to perceived provocation. It is a healthy human emotion, but when it gets out of control and turns into rage it can be destructive. Anger is a social emotion which always has a target, even if that target is God or yourself.

Anger can be active or passive. 'Active' anger includes bullying, insulting, blaming, using power, being a sore loser, not listening, violence, ignoring people's feelings, punishing, selfishness, shouting, threatening, seeking vengeance. 'Passive' anger is more subtle—the cold shoulder, gossip, fake smiles, withholding, expressing resentments behind people's backs, giving the 'silent treatment', emotional blackmail.

People with anger issues often do not want to address them. Their behaviours are so damaging that they don't want to admit their problem because of shame or fear of losing control. So a self-justification reflex sets in.

> *There was never an angry man that thought his anger unjust.*
> *Francis de Sales[46]*

As Christians we are not given the option of continual self-justification, no matter how tempting that reflex feels, nor of insisting that everyone around us learn to cope with our anger. Rather, we are asked to take responsibility for it ourselves, as we are with all sinful responses to emotion. The Bible is clear that we cannot rationalise and justify uncontrolled anger .

> *Remember this, my dear friends! Everyone must be quick to listen, but slow to speak and slow to become angry. Human anger does not achieve God's righteous purpose.*
> *James 1:19–20 (GNT)*

> *Keep your temper under control; it is foolish to harbor a grudge.*
> *Ecclesiastes 7:9 (GNT)*

But now you must get rid of all these things: anger, passion, and hateful feelings. No insults or obscene talk must ever come from your lips.
Colossians 3:8 (GNT)

REASONS FOR CHRISTIANS TO SEEK SOLUTIONS TO ANGER ISSUES

- For yourself. To avoid sin.

  If you become angry, do not let your anger lead you into sin, and do not stay angry all day... Get rid of all bitterness, passion, and anger. No more shouting or insults, no more hateful feelings of any sort.
  Ephesians 4:26, 31 (GNT)

- For others. It hurts them.

  Don't give in to worry or anger; it only leads to trouble.
  Psalm 37:8 (gnt)

- To not be a bad witness.

  But keep away from foolish and ignorant arguments; you know that they end up in quarrels. As the Lord's servant, you must not quarrel. You must be kind toward all, a good and patient teacher, who is gentle as you correct your opponents, for it may be that God will give them the opportunity to repent and come to know the truth.
  2 Timothy 2:23–25 (gnt)

- To not waste your days.

  For every minute you are angry you lose sixty seconds of happiness.

  Ralph Waldo Emerson[47]

MANAGING ANGER AS A CHRISTIAN

Listing specific strategies to manage anger is beyond the scope of this book (see Resources section to explore some of them further). One important option, however, is getting help for anger issues from a psychologist or counsellor.

For Christians, seeing a psychologist or counsellor for anger issues seems to be harder than for other issues. This may be a reaction to feeling judged as a failure. But if you have a heart problem you see a cardiologist, if you have a lung problem you see a pulmonary specialist like me—and if you have emotional issues you see a psychologist, counsellor or psychiatrist.

Getting help as a family requires courage

A psychologist can assess whether your anger is a problem, can help you determine why it is happening and can help you understand it. Together you can work out how to get what you want in a better way. They can advise you about other resources to help manage your anger (such as support groups, books and courses). They can also help you manage other problems that may be associated with anger, such as depression, violence or personal relationships.

To access a psychologist you might find it easiest to ask your family doctor, another health professional or your pastor. That is an important step in the process. To do this is not an expression of lack of faith but of love for those around you, and of willingness to change. A Christian psychologist will bring special insights, but it is not necessary that they be a person of faith.

Disappointment

Chronic disappointment is another type of suffering that Christians can experience. Disappointment due to our expectations not being met and the pain that flows from this can affect our marriage, our work, our friend-ships, our parenting and our community or church service.

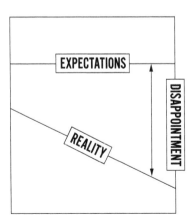

The 'disappointment gap' between expectation and reality is actually a normal part of life, and the sort of suffering it produces is an essential part of the journey. It teaches us how to see things through and push through the barriers of failure and disappointment—something success would not do. Yet the 'disappointment gap' can eat away at us day after day. Understanding the difference between *hope* and *expectation* is a very stabilising and reasonable approach to handling disappointment.

EXPECTATION CAN BE A TWO-EDGED SWORD

'If you expect nothing, you will get nothing.' We are encouraged to expect great things of ourselves and great things from God. This includes setting goals and taking risks to achieve those goals.

> *'Come,' he said. Then Peter got down out of the boat, walked on the water and came toward Jesus.*
> *Matthew 14:29*

> *Yes, risk-taking is inherently failure-prone. Otherwise, it would be called 'sure-thing-taking'.*
> *Jim McMahon[48]*

> *One does not discover new lands without consenting to lose sight of the shore for a very long time.*
> *Andre Gide[49]*

But expectation is a two-edged sword. The adventure of faithful risk-taking doesn't always turn out as we expect it to. The inspiring stories of trust and risk that work out for others may not work out for me. I expected success and got failure, and that hurts. I read about Hudson Taylor and other heroic Christian pioneers and end up feeling disappointed in myself.

> *Life is full of disappointments, but we have to take some risks. None of us can predict the future, for only God knows what's to come... Disappointments are like weeds in the garden. You can let them grow and take over your life, or you can rout them out and let the flowers sprout.*
> *Wanda E. Brunstetter*[50]

There is often a clash between expectations/outcomes and process. Outcomes are about success, but process includes learning and experiencing things along the way. It's the difference between the pleasure of hiking up a mountain and the attainment of the summit, between the flowers sitting in the vase and growing and nurturing them. It helps to let go and open your eyes to new adventures or else you may miss out on things that God has for you.

EXPECTATIONS AND 'SCOREBOARDS'

Marriage is a classic context where expectations are not met by reality. We are fed a diet of Hollywood/Cinderella stories that tell us that once we get married all will be blissful, including our sex lives. But reality is always different. Finding the richness in a life where expectations change and we grow together requires turning disappointment into something positive.

It's in marriages that expectations typically do not match reality

Work too can be a source of serious disappointments. These are not just about failing to become successful but can be as simple as feeling a bit hollow *despite* becoming successful—asking yourself, 'Is this all there is to life?' Such disappointment can stem from having a non-biblical view of success, from having your treasure in the wrong place.

> I tried so hard
> You stole my heart
> Then tore it in two.
> Now I'm falling apart
> And don't know what to do.
> *Whitney Barton*[51]

It is easy to be tyrannised by some sort of 'scoreboard'. I sometimes speak to sports coaches, and I point out that although the scoreboard on the field might measure their performance as a coach, it does not measure their performance as a person. We all have scoreboards in our lives by which we measure ourselves or let others measure us. I invite coaches to shake their finger at the scoreboard and say, 'I refuse to be tyrannised by you. I know that to some extent you measure my success as a coach, but I will not allow you to judge my success as a man.'

The gap between expectations and reality in the whole of life can be a result of using the wrong scoreboard to measure our success as people. If we are following God's leading in our work, family, friendships and community service, we will have internal measures of success as Christians, not those from other scoreboards that cause us to misunder-stand what success is—income, fame, power, prestige, promotion, nice house, new car, kids who are good at sport, kids who are smart, kids who don't get into trouble and make us look bad. We need to choose not to be held captive by scoreboards that are not in tune with God's plan for us as created, special individuals. If we don't make this choice, we run the risk of suffering disappointment.

It is a clear fact, articulated throughout the Bible, that we really only grow through suffering. We would rather growth occurred within our comfort zones, but it doesn't happen that way. Suffering related to disap-pointment is no different. Like all suffering, disappointment can be a growth-driver if we accept that God can use it for our good.

> *God makes the life fertile by disappointments, as he makes*
> *the ground fertile by frosts.*
> *Henry Ward Beecher*[52]

Everyone experiences conflict, anger and disappointment in life. This chapter relates to situations where these are excessive and produce suffering. Most of these fly under the radar in churches because of their hidden nature and the reluctance of sufferers to discuss them with others or their pastor. But all of them can be turned around if you are willing to try. I encourage you to do so, understanding that this may be hard for you.

Key points

CONFLICT

- Conflicts are inevitable in every sphere of life.
- The keys to resolution are in the words *grace* and *truth*.
- Don't assume every conflict is resolvable.
- Don't assume every person in a conflict will be reasonable.
- Protect yourself from the negativity, anxiety and disillusionment that can occur when others don't follow the teaching and example of Jesus.

ANGER

- Anger is a normal emotion involving a hostile response to perceived provocation.
- It is only a problem when excessive, repeated or expressed in unhealthy ways.
- Anger creates problems in personal relationships, including for Christians.
- Christians are often reluctant to discuss anger issues with their pastor.
- Anger expends a lot of energy in wasted self-justification
- Christians cannot demand that others 'just learn to deal with my volatility'.
- It is tempting to feel self-righteous if your anger is not active in verbal or physical actions, but passive anger is also hurtful.

DISAPPOINTMENT

- The gap between expectations and reality is a normal part of life.
- This gap can create suffering in all parts of life.
- Expectations of ourselves and God, and taking risks, are faith-filled positions.
- Misunderstanding 'success' can lead to being tyrannised by external validation (a 'scoreboard').
- We can easily use the wrong scoreboard to measure our success as people.
- Disappointments can be growth-drivers.

PART 4

Growing From Suffering

CHAPTER 11

Growing from the grief of suffering

Grief, after the initial shock of loss, comes in waves... When you're driving alone in your car, while you're doing the dishes, while you're getting ready for work... All of a sudden it hits you how very much you miss someone, and your breath catches, and your tears flow, and the sadness is so great that it's physically painful.
Nicole Gabert[53]

Grief is an inevitable consequence of most forms of suffering. The purpose of this chapter is to focus on grief, what it means and how we can grow from it rather than being permanently disabled by it.

Surviving and growing from suffering often involves a period of grief—sometimes deep and inescapable grief that occupies all our thoughts and makes it hard to get out of bed each day.

All humans experience grief. We have always lived with it as a species. In past generations half of the children born died young, and adults died early from disease, war or accident. Children fear the death of a loving grandparent and then it happens. We live with grief in our hearts.

Grief is awful, but it can also be strangely helpful. At a minimum it reminds us that life is temporary, and being reminded of that, we don't charge on assuming that everything lasts forever. We sense that our days are numbered, and this wisdom can drive us to seize those days and live life now without postponement.

> *Teach us to number our days, that we may gain a heart of wisdom.*
> *Psalm 90:12*

Grief is mainly about loss. It may be the loss of a life (such as a loved one who has died), the loss of an expected future (such as when a child becomes disabled) or the loss of a life partner (in divorce). It may be the loss of a job, health, an ability or a dream. Whatever it is, that loss is a consequence of suffering, and every type of suffering contains some grief.

Grief can attack not only the person suffering but also their family, friends and the church communities in which they live. The journey can be easier for Christians, but a loss is a loss, and an empty heart filled with sadness is what it is and should be acknowledged without guilt.

> But for now I have to wait,
> Until we meet again.
> You will always be in my heart and thoughts,
> My dear Mum and best friend.
> Always and Forever,
> Your baby girl loves you so much.
> Ranja Kujala[54]

The roller coaster of emotions in grief tends to occur in stages. It is worth discussing those stages to help you think through how they might apply to your own life.

The stages of grief

Dr Elizabeth Kübler-Ross famously described five 'stages' of grief. Of course, it is not as simple as five discrete stages, and it would be a mistake to imagine that every person will progress sequentially from one stage to another. Some of the five stages are just different types of dominant response, and they don't always occur in everybody and certainly not always in the same order. But they are a helpful guide.

THE FIVE CLASSICAL STAGES OF GRIEF

Denial - Anger - Bargaining
Depression - Acceptance

1. Denial. Denial helps the individual cope with the initial shock of loss (such as hearing the bad news of cancer). It enables them to survive feeling overwhelmed by a sense of grief, the meaninglessness of the future and the senselessness of even continuing to try. Moving through denial allows the sufferer and others around them to accept the reality of the grief, and is an important beginning of the healing process and the journey of loss.

This applies to believers and non-believers alike. When it is the sufferer's family or friends in denial, this should not be confused with a lack of faith or caring on their part.

> *Most of church was in denial when our young pastor got terminal cancer, even when he was totally wasted away, bed-bound, breathless and obviously had only a few days to live. They didn't want the more rational, realistic church members to talk to him or his family. The nursing staff actually begged his doctors to talk some sense into his parishioners and his friends so they would face the reality that he was dying. Some of his congregation even insisted on visitors sterilizing their hands when they came to see him in his last days so that 'he would not get an infection when he was miraculously healed'.*
> *Anonymous*

2. Anger. Expressing anger if it is there (and it usually is to some extent) is also important. Other emotions such as frustration and anxiety may intrude, but anger is common.

Anger is frequently directed at others—in the case of illness or disability, at doctors, nurses and hospitals; in the case of divorce, at the partner and friends; in the case of unemployment, at the workplace and colleagues. Often it is directed at family .

Friends, pastors and doctors can end up for a while in the firing line because of the temptation to 'shoot the messenger', and this can be hard for them. Hearing the honest truth is difficult to take, and these 'messengers' can be accused of being 'brutal' simply because the truth is hard. But lies and euphemisms turn out to be more brutal—I have seen that many times.

> But my mind is racing with 'what if'
> Why can't cancer end like a fairytale or even be
> a myth
> Somebody please take this sorrow
> It's too late
> Time does not wait
> Shavon Mcclendon[55]

Anger can also be directed at God. 'Why did God let this happen to me?' 'Why is he letting me suffer when my family needs me?' 'Doesn't he know I have a major ministry developing?' God is an ideal target for anger, and in fact the Bible encourages us to express anger towards him, as in the Psalms:

How long, O LORD? Will you forget me forever?
   How long will you hide your face from me?
How long must I wrestle with my thoughts
   and every day have sorrow in my heart?
   How long will my enemy triumph over me?
Look on me and answer, O LORD my God.
Psalm 13

Anger is about pain and a sense of helplessness. Suppressing it adds an unnecessary burden, so it is important to express those feelings—but in helpful ways that do not damage others.

3. Depression. As these initial responses pass and the truth sinks in, it is easy to start to feel empty. A deep sense of resignation and grief can enter, leading to a depressive stage that goes on and on. This can be an appropriate response to great loss, and it is not a sign of mental illness unless it is severe and prolonged.

> *With each passing day the house becomes more and more silent as Ciara's death drains the life from it and I am drawn further and further into my world of darkness. The torpor of grief takes over. I have no interest in anything.*
> *Una Glennon[56]*

At this stage people may experience grief and sadness beyond anything they ever imagined. It may feel like it will last forever and that there is no point in going on. This is natural and not something you can just snap out of. Faith too might suffer, either temporarily or permanently.

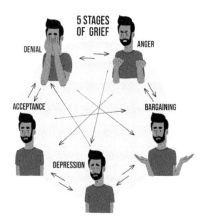

The five stages of grief

All this can become complicated, and many people (especially Christians) can be tempted to wear a fake smile. Or in the case of severe illness, they might tell others only small bits of good news despite the doctor saying that things overall are getting worse and the illness is progressing.

> *I would also advise any couples that are facing the death of one of the partners that it's okay to be sad. It really is. It's not a sign of lack of faith. I cried every night after Paul died for about a year and a half... I still cry sometimes when I'm talking to friends who knew him.*
> *Judith Curtis*

4. Bargaining. Bargaining can only happen if there is someone to bargain with. Believers commonly want to bargain with God. 'If you'll just allow my wife to get over her breast cancer/bring my husband back to me/heal my son from his disability, I will ...' 'Please take me instead of my son.' 'I will become a full-time missionary if you will let my daughter live.'

This is a very difficult position to be in as it creates enormous uncertainty. It is actually another form of denial or avoidance and can create a lot of 'if only's'.

5. Acceptance. This stage is about accepting the reality of the loss. You are still not happy with things, but they are what they are. It is just the way life is for you now. It does not mean that you are all right with that reality, just that you have accepted it.

Acceptance happens a bit at a time because grief is a long process. I think it is generally easier for Christians, at least when it comes to terminal disease—we know where we are going. However, I have seen Christians clinging white-knuckled to life and refusing to accept the obvious and non-believers come to a beautiful acceptance of their fate that allows for grace and dying well.

Taking enough time to grieve

One of the challenges facing those who grieve can be the 'hurry up' comments received from others. I have seen this in the context of death, divorce and other losses. Often Christians expect people to 'live victoriously', which is a huge pressure and can add to someone's sense of guilt, shame and failure that they're not moving on. We can expect this of ourselves too. This chapter should help give you permission to take your time.

Sometimes an individual may move on reasonably quickly, especially if they have had time to process their grief in advance, (for example, if their loved one has had cancer for some time). But whatever the loss—death, divorce, disability, unemployment or something else—it can take a long time. People in grief don't need to hear unhelpful phrases such as 'It's time to get back to life' or 'It's been two years now and you should stop crying and move on.' Sometimes it takes way more than two years—it might take ten. Everyone is different. If God has gifted you with a person you loved deeply and they are gone, give yourself permission to take as long as it takes. Don't expect simply to wake up one day free of grief.

Grief can continue for a long time

As long as you are processing your grief and not avoiding it and retreating, you can get through it and grow from it, even if it doesn't seem like it.

> *After my husband Paul died of his brain tumour, I cried every night for about 18 months. Then during the day I would get up and go to parent–teacher meetings and other things that I just had to do. But at night I would cry. People thought I was really strong because during the day I wasn't falling about crying, but in reality I was crying every night.*
> **Judith Curtis**

Grief in families. Within families, some members take longer to grieve than others, and each person will grieve differently. This can sometimes cause tensions.

Each family member grieves in their own way and their own time

It is common to try to avoid the cause of grief, to look the other way. I once visited a cousin in England whose husband had dropped dead on a golf course. As we talked, she started to get a bit weepy, but her adult daughter told her not to talk about it because it only brought on tears. Such a shame—talking with me, as someone who knew her late husband, would have helped her a lot. It is important to celebrate the good and not hide from the memories.

We don't mind discussing Paul since he died, reflecting on his life. We talk about how grateful we are for having had him in our lives... To anyone else who is facing the tragedy of a partner who is going to die I would suggest that you step back and think about the wonderful life you've had to that point, but also remember that this life is tiny compared to eternity...

*That sounds glib, but we are here to serve God and bring glory
to him in our lives, whether we are widows, widowers, single
or whatever. And that includes when we are grieving. And how
we do that influences and encourages others.*
Judith Curtis

Failing to grieve can make you bitter rather than better

Taking an extended time to go through the valley of grief may be appropriate, but it is also easy to get stuck in the valley, to be totally absorbed by your sadness or anger. This can leave you with an enormous feeling of bitterness, frustration and anxiety.

It is well known in medical circles that *grief handled badly makes people bitter, but grief handled well makes people better.*

Understanding and responding to this concept can have a dramatic effect on the future. The principle applies to believers as well as non-believers. I am sure you know people, including Christians, who remain self-absorbed in their suffering so that it occupies their every thought and conversation.

This is common—journalists on the evening news always find someone who is bitter about what they have experienced, angrily blaming the hospitals, the doctors, the police, the government or God.

> ## THE 'PRISON OF BITTERNESS' IS USUALLY DOMINATED BY ONE WORD: BLAME

This is the 'prison of bitterness'. It is usually dominated by one word: *blame*. Whatever loss has triggered the grief, there will be reasons for it, and those reasons are worth knowing—but only to help the sufferer understand the present more clearly. That understanding can be a springboard to eventually moving on, but it is a problem if it becomes a focus for anger and resentment. When that happens, grief can become the person's regular talking point, their mission and even their identity.

> *Acrid bitterness inevitably seeps into the lives of people who harbor grudges and suppress anger, and bitterness is always a poison. It keeps your pain alive instead of letting you deal with it and get beyond it. Bitterness sentences you to relive the hurt over and over.*
> *Lee Strobel*[57]

One characteristic of people who are locked in a prison of bitterness is their continual looking backwards in anger and frustration. That is why God asks us, as he did Job, to spend limited time looking backwards and to focus more on looking forward to how we will get through it and be transformed in the process.

People stuck in bitterness also tend to 'listen' to themselves rather than 'talk' to themselves. Whatever thoughts they have about their suffering drive their emotional responses ('Why me?' 'I'm never going to be able to get through this.' 'This isn't fair.' 'What did I do to deserve this?') We handle our suffering better if we start talking to ourselves rather than just listening to those clamouring internal voices.

Living in bitterness and blame actually extends suffering. Distressing emotions feed back and increase the level of irritability, fear, anger, frustration, guilt, loneliness and anxiety. Feelings of hopelessness and helplessness become worse. It is possible to get locked into the secondary pain of grief in ways that remove aspirations for growth. We can hang on to grief and continue seeking people's empathy, repeatedly telling our story to anyone who will listen and not letting it go. This can mean being arrested in that stage, unable to grow.

> *Some friends of mine won't allow their children to celebrate Christmas. That is because their son died at Christmas time and they are too sad and bitter about it. And that was ten years ago. They are stuck in their grief.*
> *Adeline Sylvester[58]*

ESCAPING THE PRISON OF BITTERNESS

The good news is that the door of the prison of bitterness is not locked. We only remain imprisoned if we fail to push the door open and walk out.

I would hate to sound trite here, as if this were easy. I know it is not. I have watched grief eat away at people, filling their thoughts from dawn to midnight, creating clutching feelings of anxiety in their chest, breaking up marriages and destroying friendships. If your experience is anything like that, I feel deeply for you and weep with you. Sometimes we struggle to grow from the journey of suffering because of the sheer weight of the loss and grief. It may be too early to expect growth—it can't be hurried under such circumstances.

Yet I have seen the change happen many times. I have seen families get locked in a cycle of bitterness towards each other or someone else, but with open sharing, weeping together, honesty, sometimes with professional/experienced help, they have been transformed into families who laugh and love and are strengthened by their grief, and who grow from it in wisdom and compassion for others.

Locked in the 'prison of bitterness'

The phrase 'what doesn't kill you makes you stronger' is not necessarily true. For suffering to make you better, you have to be active in the process, or what doesn't kill you can actually make you weaker. Victor Frankl, who survived a Nazi concentration camp, describes in his book *Man's Search for Meaning* how his captors removed from him everything of value, including his dignity. All that remained was his freedom to choose how to respond—and he chose to respond beyond what was being done to him. That power of response, our power to choose, is what enables us to seek growth from suffering and freedom beyond the prison of bitterness.

> **Myth:** What doesn't kill you makes you stronger.
>
> **Reality:** Whether it makes you stronger or weaker depends on how you choose to respond.

In our suffering and grief we can angrily recoil from God. God understands those who fume and shout—in fact, that is probably a healthy sign, a place to start. But in responding to suffering, it is our attitude that will determine the outcome. The way forward it to lose our unhealthy self-absorption, to die to self and to allow growth and service of others.

> *Very truly I tell you, unless a kernel of wheat falls to the ground and dies, it remains only a single seed. But if it dies, it produces many seeds.*
> *John 12:24*

> *Life is like photography. We develop from the negatives.*
> *Jason McNaughten[59]*

All of this can be hardest of all in on-going or long-term grief, such as the grief associated with permanent disability, mental illness or chronic drug addiction. The grief of death can diminish over the years, but in these situations grief can be a constant companion. It's then not just a matter of getting through it to 'the other side'—there is no other side. It's not just about breaking out of the prison of sadness and bitterness, but staying out of it.

My son might have died, and it is sad, but after 10 years we are moving on. But you die every day.
Anonymous. (Father of dead Hollywood actor, addressing another father whose son has a 20-year methamphetamine addiction)

Strategies for growing from suffering

Growing from suffering and grief requires intentionality, choices and decisions. I have found two practical strategies very helpful in my own journey to move on in the journey of suffering.

CHRISTIAN MINDFULNESS

When I am suffering, I find that I replay my concerns in my mind over and over again. This intrusive thinking tends to make me even more worried and miserable.

What has helped me enormously through this is learning Christian 'mindfulness'.

Mindfulness in general is wonderful in that it helps us be still. The added value of Christian mindfulness is that it tries to get us to speak less and listen more to God—to 'be still and know that I am God' (Ps 46:10). Focusing on God's nature is a powerful way to walk each day of suffering. These are truths that can be embraced despite uncertainty, exhaustion and frustration.

> **FAITH CAN SWIM WHERE REASON CAN ONLY WADE**

When I combine mindfulness with the Diamond Meditation (chapter 3), it helps me to reach out and take God's hand to climb out of the valley of suffering. I'm reminded that there are rewards available to the Christian on the other side of grief, such as insight, compassion, capacity for intimacy, and a greater ability to help and inspire others. Faith can swim where reason can only wade.

> *Christian mindfulness includes paying attention, doing one thing at a time, and refraining from 'future tripping' and 'baggage carrying.' Paying attention requires both effort and trust. The effort comes in choosing to 'set your mind on things above' (Colossians 3:2) and 'renew your mind' (Romans 12:2).*
> *Dallas Willard*[60]

THE SOCK STRATEGY

It can be hard to move on and grow from suffering and grief if you keep doing what you have always done. That means changing, and change is hard.

Over the years I have come to see that there are almost invariably four major obstacles to change. First, we can *deny* the problem and the need for change. Second, we can *blame* someone or something other than ourselves. Third, we can *procrastinate*, finding excuses not to act. Fourth, we can *relapse,* falling back into old ways of thinking through busyness, distraction, lack of accountability or simply lack of focus.

A particular strategy that has helped many people change is what I call the SOCK strategy. SOCK stands for See, Own, Change and Keep

It Up. These four steps directly address the four common obstacles to change.

See (rather than deny)

Own (rather than blame)

Change (rather than procrastinate)

Keep it up (rather than relapse)

These four steps correspond directly to core truths about change in the Christian life: face the truth, confess, repent and persevere.

Understanding these four obstacles makes it possible to see where someone (particularly yourself) is blocked in escaping the prison of bitterness. This knowledge gives them a start in getting past that block. For example, more 'education' (nagging) about the need to change might help if someone is blocked at S, but if they are blocked at O, C or K it will just generate more guilt.

Here are some specific SOCK actions that can help you get out of the prison of bitterness and onto the path to growth.

1. **See** the suffering and understand it. Examine it and the reasons for it. Stop avoiding it. Ask others for input if you are in denial. Understand the emotions you are feeling and accept them for what they are. Indeed, embrace them—in the end they will be your friends, because as you express them they will become part of the driving force for your transformation.

2. **Own** what is happening to you, how you think about it and what you can do about it. You may not be able to change the suffering, but you can change your response to it. Decide that you are going to take responsibility for your part in the partnership with God, and don't just expect him to do everything.

3. **Change** the things you can and let go of the things you can't. Don't postpone taking the first steps, but also don't put yourself under pressure with unrealistic timelines and steps that are too large. Make them single steps, and make them small and achievable. Then plan the next steps. In setting off to take these steps, take God's hand. This is a partnership and you need him.

4. To help you **keep your change up**, post reminder notes to yourself on your bathroom mirror, or write them in your electronic calendar with recurring reminders. Generate ways to be held accountable, involving others (professional or otherwise). Read about and meditate on 'pressing on' (Phil 3:10–16), enduring (Heb 12:1; 1 Cor 10:13) and the unseen purposes behind suffering (2 Cor 4:18; Rom 8:28–29). Ask God what you are meant to learn from all that you are experiencing (Jas 1:5).

God's part and ours

Some Christians rely purely on prayer, asking God to solve all their problems. They seem to want him to take over the journey for them, like a pilot or cab driver. That sounds super-spiritual, but we can sometimes use prayer as avoidance: instead of going on a diet, we ask God to fix our over-eating; we pray earnestly for our kids but only do the bare minimum in spending one-on-one time with them and learning best-practice parenting skills.

Prayer is necessary but rarely sufficient. God invites us into a partnership

Prayer is necessary, but it is not sufficient. If prayer alone were enough, Paul's pastoral letters would have been only a few paragraphs long, simply asking people to pray more. Of course, we must pray, and God will do his bit. But he asks and expects us to be part of this partnership. When we suffer, he puts his hand out in unconditional love, but we can knock it away and decline. If we do, he will still not let us be destroyed, but we will have trouble moving out of the prison of bitterness and into growth.

Suffering is not intrinsically good, but God can make it work for good in the future, provided you join in this partnership. You are invited to choose your future by placing your hand in his, letting your bitterness die and allowing yourself the freedom to grow, bloom and be fruitful.

> *And we know that in all things God works for the good of those who love him, who have been called according to his purpose.*
> *Romans 8:28*
>
> *When you go through deep waters, I will be with you.*
> *Isaiah 43:2*

This chapter has talked about strategies for handling the grief of suffering. If it is you who are grieving, don't feel that you need to do these things until you are ready. I don't want to make you feel worse than you do, more guilty than you already feel. When the time is right, you might find the ideas in this chapter helpful. I encourage you to meditate on them and to find a community of friends who will love you and share your journey in compassion and concern.

Key points

- Grief is about loss, whether it be due to death, divorce, unemployment or some other cause.
- Understanding the typical phases of grief prepares you for them.
- Grief handled badly can make you *bitter*; grief handled well can make you *better*.
- Growing from suffering involves a partnership between you and God.

CHAPTER 12

Turning suffering into service

Your greatest ministry will most likely come out of your greatest hurt.
Rick Warren

Some people are paralysed or emotionally disabled by suffering. But the Christian message is clear: we can grow from suffering and in the process better serve God, sacrificially. The purpose of this chapter is to explore how that can happen.

An old Chinese tale tells of a woman whose son had died. She was overwhelmed with grief. A holy man advised her that to heal her sorrow she needed to find a mustard seed in a home that had never known sorrow. The woman went from house to house, asking if that home had never known sorrow. Because sorrow is ubiquitous, she did not find a single home that had not known it. But as she went from house to house, she stayed and comforted her hosts a little. Finally she realised that the act of providing comfort to others who were suffering had driven her own sorrow from her life.

Service to others as an outcome of suffering

Most of this book has been about the personal journey of victims, families, friends and communities when somebody suffers. This final chapter discusses the turning of personal suffering into service that helps others who suffer. It is not a chapter for those in the acute phase of suffering (for example, those who have just found out that they or their loved one has cancer or that their child has just drowned). Such times are too raw and devastating to begin thinking about turning that suffering into service. The chapter is for those who have been through a period of suffering and want to think about what to do next.

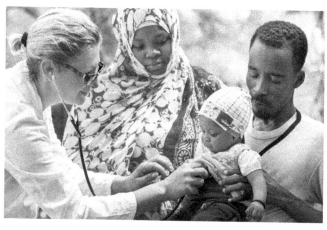

Service to the needy helps everyone, including those growing from suffering

Turning suffering into service is a deeply Christian activity. Its benefits extend beyond the sufferers who are served—it also benefits the person who is serving and embodies and promotes the gospel. Further, showing compassion to others is a helpful way to escape from the prison of bitterness and sorrow. This can be surprising to those who feel that their sorrow has sapped their energy and volition and that they just want it assuaged. Compassionate service actually has a curious way of doing that. Maybe you know people who have turned their suffering into service and have seen the passion and meaning this has given them.

> *Let each of you look not only to his own interests, but also to*
> *the interests of others.*
> *Philippians 2:4 (ESV)*

Suffering in life can uncover untold depths of character and unknown strength for service. People who go through life unscathed by sorrow and untouched by pain tend to

be shallow in their perspectives on life. Suffering, on the other hand, tends to plow up the surface of our lives to uncover the depths that provide greater strength of purpose and accomplishment. Only deeply plowed earth can yield bountiful harvests.
Billy Graham[61]

Turning suffering into service is a choice

Turning suffering into compassionate service is not automatic. Some people choose to remain in the prison of bitterness. For others, exhaustion from suffering makes them want to opt out, to just sit down and live in a zone of comfort, enjoying having survived their time of trial. I can appreciate that and I don't judge it—the emotional, physical and social price paid for surviving suffering can be great. Just getting through each day can remain a challenge.

> **SERVICE TURNS OUR TRIALS INTO SOMETHING OF MEANING AND BENEFIT FOR OTHERS**

My point is not to shout at you like a football coach to get up off your chair and serve others. I would not be so harsh. It is to help you realise that the reason God has asked us to turn our suffering into service is because it is a way of turning our trials into something of meaning and benefit to others. That is the way God has set things up, and that is why he has given us the second greatest commandment: *'Love your neighbor as yourself'* *(Lk 10:27).*

Because of our son being severely disabled we have been invited to give talks on suffering and have been able to share with others in ways that have helped them. I've become more confident to talk about the suffering of my disabled child and my husband. I'm never sure about just how much I've helped others when I share my suffering. But I trust that God has used me in that way.
Judith Curtis

I still sometimes wake up at night and shake my head at some of the things that happened in our church leadership meetings. Although things said by the key offender were ridiculous and patently untrue, they still got to me. But I am grateful for all the things I have learned during that period, and how that time of unquestionable suffering has brought me closer to God... I am now in a position where I can talk to others and it has helped them cope with their similar situations. Indeed, when I mention my struggles I find that many others have experienced similar conflicts in leadership. I admit that I am amazed at how often this sort of thing happens in churches.
Anonymous

The heart of compassionate service

At the heart of the notion of compassionate service is Jesus' story of the Good Samaritan. He told the story in response to a question: 'Who is my neighbour?' (Lk 10:29).

I was confronted with this exact challenge when I began writing this book. I had organised a week off work to sit down at my computer with my notes and start pulling it together. Somewhat ritually, I depowered my work computer at 5 pm on Friday night and headed home, relieved that I had the whole upcoming week to work on the book. An hour later, at 6.02 pm, a magnitude 7.5 earthquake hit Central Sulawesi and sent a tsunami smashing into the town of Palu, destroying buildings, killing more than 5000, injuring 10,000 more and creating more than 200,000 refugees.

Of course I was moved with compassion when I heard this—those people were my neighbours. But I knew that I could not help in those first few days. It was the local Indonesian disaster response teams that would be most important early on, and it would probably be impossible to get into the disaster zone to help anyway. So over the weekend I began writing my book. By Monday I could not continue because I read the story of the Good Samaritan again and felt like a hypocrite, passing by on the opposite side of the road. Sulawesi was a neighbour, across the ocean from the state where I live. What should love for my neighbour look like?

I particularly felt this because I knew I could help. I had the disaster response medical training and experience plus the Indonesian language skills. So putting my pen down, I contacted my Indonesian disaster relief colleagues, was told I was needed and headed north to serve in one of the most gruelling disaster relief situations I have worked in.

That made the parable of the Good Samaritan deeply personal to me. Perhaps I would have finished this book a lot earlier if I hadn't 'crossed the road' to love my neighbour. But then I would have had an inescapable feeling that I was talking the talk without walking the walk.

Learning from the Good Samaritan

The parable in Luke 10 tells us a lot about the attitude we need to have towards opportunities for service.

> *A man was going down from Jerusalem to Jericho, when he was attacked by robbers. They stripped him of his clothes, beat him and went away, leaving him half dead.*

The Samaritan was not looking for someone to help. The beaten traveller just appeared before him on his journey. We don't need to cross oceans and go to disaster zones to find people who are suffering—they are all around us. As I said earlier, if you scratch the surface of anyone approaching or beyond middle age, you will find suffering. Your choice is whether to cross the road and provide compassionate service or pass by on the other side.

> YOU DON'T NEED TO CROSS OCEANS TO DISASTER ZONES TO FIND PEOPLE WHO ARE SUFFERING

IT IS EASY TO FIND EXCUSES NOT TO DO ANYTHING

A priest happened to be going down the same road, and when he saw the man, he passed by on the other side. So too, a Levite, when he came to the place and saw him, passed by on the other side.

It is easy to find reasons for doing nothing. To be fair, many of these are quite logical and responsible. It is not possible to respond to every need that confronts us—that is a recipe for burnout and family neglect.

But there are excuses that generate avoidance. Sometimes I wonder if the priest passed by, continued on to his synagogue and then offered up a prayer for the wounded man.

To understand this, it is helpful to consider what a *bad* Samaritan looks like. I experienced exactly that when I was studying at the Liverpool School of Tropical Medicine in England many years ago. I was a relatively poor young doctor at the time, renting a room in a house in a suburb of Liverpool called Green Lane and driving an old Ford Cortina that I bought for about $200.

Early one evening my car failed to start because the battery was flat. The man who lived next door had parked his car right in front of mine and by coincidence walked out of his house just as I was wondering what to do. So I asked him politely if I could jumpstart my car from his battery. It would take no more than five minutes. (I admit that I looked pretty scruffy at the time—longish hair, jeans, T-shirt and bare feet. But I was polite!)

Unbelievably, he said he was sorry but he could not help because he was 'heading to a prayer meeting in downtown Liverpool and would be late'.

I was aghast. It was particularly upsetting to me because this occurred during the two years when I was living in rejection of the church. I went upstairs, found my landlady's Bible and wrote out the parable of the Good Samaritan on a piece of paper. I replaced the words 'Jerusalem' with 'Green Lane' and 'Jericho' with 'Liverpool', then changed 'attacked by robbers' to 'had a car with a flat battery that needed a jumpstart'. I finished with the phrase 'whatever you do to the least of my brethren, you do to me'.

I folded the note, walked next door and slipped it under his front door. Maybe he prayed for me at his prayer meeting, I don't know—I never heard from him again. He did not knock on my door to apologise, nor did he write a note in reply.

> ## PRAYER IS NOT MEANT TO BE A WAY TO ESCAPE ACTION

It was somewhat ironic that this man used prayer as his escape clause. It is not uncommon to see Christians using faith and prayer as a way of avoiding doing something. We feel more spiritual if we 'pray first'. When I feel myself doing this, I'm particularly challenged by the New Testament's description of genuine love:

> *If I have a faith that can move mountains, but do not have love, I am nothing.*
> *1 Corinthians 13:2*

> *What good is it, my brothers and sisters, if someone claims to have faith but has no deeds? Can such faith save them? Suppose a brother or a sister is without clothes and daily food. If one of you says to them, 'Go in peace; keep warm and well fed,' but does nothing about their physical needs,*

what good is it? In the same way, faith by itself, if it is not accompanied by action, is dead.
James 2:14–17

Sometimes now, when the 'let's-pray-first' reflex occurs in a group, I try to be a bit disruptive and suggest we *don't* pray first but go and do something to help first. We can pray during or after the helping.

Use the gifts and opportunities you have to serve. Another excuse is to say that you don't have any skills to help. But the Good Samaritan reminds us that everyone has the ability to reach out in empathy. Some gifts are more obviously helpful in certain situations (for example, medical skills in a disaster zone). But God calls us to faithfully use the gifts he has given us, and he will take care of the job of making them useful.

An example of this occurred when I met the well-known Christian singer Darlene Zschech, whose songs 'Shout to the Lord', 'Worthy Is the Lamb' and over a hundred others have inspired many. She asked me about the disaster relief work I had done Indonesia. Then she said, 'That's wonderful—you get to really help, but all I do is sing.'

Darlene Zschech—an example of understanding and using your gifts and not envying others

This surprised me, so I told her a story I heard from our project director in post-tsunami Aceh. He was sitting in the wings of a US Christian TV station, waiting to be interviewed about the relief work, and got talking to a young woman sitting beside him. He asked her name, and she said, 'Darlene Zschech, from Australia.' He immediately said, 'Darlene, I need to thank you. Your songs helped me get through a very dark period in my life.' If she hadn't followed her calling and used her gift of singing, she wouldn't have been able to help him, and perhaps he wouldn't have been able to run a huge disaster relief program that assisted hundreds of thousands of people.

When Darlene interviewed me recently from the podium at her church north of Sydney, I reminded her publicly of that story. I encouraged the congregation to understand that everyone has the capacity to give empathy, to show the compassion of Jesus. When it comes to service, everyone's gift can be useful. Don't assume that because you are not a doctor, nurse, engineer or airline pilot your gifts or opportunities are any less significant. Just be faithful to those gifts.

SERVING REQUIRES SOME RISK

> *But a Samaritan, as he traveled, came where the man was; and when he saw him, he took pity on him. He went to him and bandaged his wounds, pouring on oil and wine. Then he put the man on his own donkey, brought him to an inn and took care of him.*

One thing that strikes me about the Good Samaritan parable—and I admit I was slow to see this—is that the Samaritan took an incredible risk. How was he to know that the robbers were not hiding, waiting to pounce on anyone who stopped to help? That is possibly why the others didn't stop. With his donkey and what he was carrying (wine, oil and sufficient money to pay for the care of the wounded man), he was a sitting duck. He probably mulled this over in his mind before crossing the road. But cross the road he did.

Turning suffering into compassionate service is not free of risk. In fact, faith demands risk. When Peter stepped out of the boat, he could have drowned. It was a risk. In chapter 1 I told the story of 'Twink's Map', how a young couple took a risk by going with their children to serve the poor in Thailand. That risk cost the lives of the wife and two of their children. Christians have faced these sorts of risks every day for the past 2000 years. It's just not possible to live in cotton wool.

> ## THE GOOD SAMARITAN TOOK AN INCREDIBLE RISK
> ## WHEN HE CROSSED THE ROAD TO HELP

Work in disaster response areas involves facing significant risk to life—communicable diseases, credible terrorist threats, driving at speed for long distances on damaged roads near landslides, flying around in helicopters and fixed-wing planes that have to land wherever they can. The more personal risks that impact individuals can be utterly exhausting—long travel times, oppressive heat and humidity, long days of hard work in difficult circumstances, speaking in a foreign language all day, and then getting up the next morning to do it all over again. Service is not risk-free, but we are called to step out of our comfort zone and be willing to take risks to serve God. Faith requires courage; it is not a means of escaping fear and risk.

Have I not commanded you? Be strong and courageous. Do not be afraid; do not be discouraged, for the LORD your God will be with you wherever you go.
Joshua 1:9

So do not fear, for I am with you; do not be dismayed, for I am your God. I will strengthen you and help you.
Isaiah 41:10

If we walk away from risk to keep ourselves safe, we will waste our lives.
John Piper[62]

The dangers of life are infinite, and among them is safety.
Goethe[63]

SERVING INVOLVES SOME COST

The next day he took out two denarii and gave them to the innkeeper. 'Look after him,' he said, 'and when I return, I will reimburse you for any extra expense you may have.'

Service also requires a willingness to pay a cost. That may be a cost in time, treasure or talents. For the Good Samaritan, it meant time out of his journey to help the wounded man and the cost of a substantial sum of money.

Everybody I know who has sacrificially turned their suffering into compassionate service to others has paid those same prices. They have sacrificed time and they have sacrificed income. Yet I have seen, time and time again, where this sacrifice becomes trivial compared with the benefits of service. I have watched doctors agonise over the cost of giving up work time to join a group that is helping the needy, yet at the end of those weeks be so inspired that they ask when they can do it again. Serving often induces a spectacular change in them, a recalibration of life. But they have to choose up front to pay the cost. If they do not, they will never realise how wonderful it is to provide sacrificial compassionate service.

The emotional costs of service. It is important to acknowledge that there is often an emotional cost as well. This is crucial to consider, because if you have suffered personally, you may not be as emotionally robust as you might otherwise have been. Understanding the emotional cost of service, and mechanisms of optimal self-care, is vital.

Both as a doctor breaking the devastating news of terminal illness to cancer patients and in my work in disaster zones, I have experienced the emotional costs of service. I am sometimes asked, 'Bruce, how do you personally survive that? It must be hard on you.' It is.

When I first arrived in Aceh after the 2004 Indian Ocean tsunami, it was difficult to take in the level of destruction. Buildings were razed for several kilometres from the ocean, roads were blocked, boats were dumped way inland and debris was everywhere. But it was the personal level of tragedy that touched my heart. Kettles and smashed tricycles lying in the mud and clothing hanging from destroyed buildings made me realise what must have happened to countless families as the wave swamped them.

Clothes, tricycles and a kettle —stark reminders of the mothers and children killed and families devastated. Examples of the added emotional toll of serving in areas of need.

It was emotionally gruelling. I felt a black cloud of sadness everywhere. There was almost no colour in any of the few markets open for business. Survivors mostly wore grim faces of grief and broken-heartedness or gave forced half-smiles.

I did not initially talk to our patients about their tsunami experiences—it did not seem right. However, we found that survivors were not sharing their feelings of grief and loss with each other. That was partly cultural and partly because everyone had lost somebody and no one wanted to engage in a 'tragedy competition'. They also wanted to avoid being disappointed by the lack of empathy from others who were also suffering.

Remaining stoically silent like this was unhealthy for people, so we changed our approach. We started asking patients about what they had gone through. Many of their experiences were horrendous and the stories difficult to hear. They sometimes left us weeping afterwards.

This kind of experience leaves its mark. And yet, in a strange way, I feel that the emotional cost of compassionate service is an essential part of the growth that flows from it. This is the irony we saw earlier in the book—that we only really grow from hardship and suffering. Certainly I have grown from the emotional hardships of service.

Jesus makes it clear that staying in our comfort zone does not fulfil his second commandment:

> 'Which of these three do you think was a neighbor to the man who fell into the hands of robbers?' The expert in the law replied, 'The one who had mercy on him.' Jesus told him, 'Go and do likewise.'

How turning suffering into service can help you personally

It can surprise people to learn that sacrificial service can help the server as much as it helps those who are served. It's easy to think of it as a one-way street—a strong, helpful servant reaches out to a helpless person in need. But God has wonderful gifts available to those who serve.

You gain greater peace, insight and wisdom. I was once on a train travelling between Seattle and Vancouver and sat with a Californian woman during dinner. As we chatted, she told me that her son had died of a drug overdose. She admitted that both she and her husband had overworked and hadn't 'been there' for their son. She described the devastating effect of his death on them.

I said I was a little surprised that she was able to speak about it so openly. If it had been me, I may well have broken down in tears.

She replied that she still felt sad when she talked about it, but what got her and her husband through the suffering was joining a group of parents who had undergone similar tragedies. They were able to support each other. Then she was invited to lead a group, then another, and now she travelled around to other cities providing help to parents in similar situations. She said it was only that process of turning her own suffering into care for others that had enabled her to deal with her sorrow, grow from it and talk about it with strength rather than trying to avoid talking about it at all.

When you turn your suffering into service, it can help you deal with the memories of your own suffering. Rather than forgetting your own suffering, sacrificial service can help you deal with those memories and speak of them in strength rather than weakness. It helps you deal with your own sorrow.

Through service you also get greater insight, wisdom and skills about how to care for and comfort other people who are suffering. This can help make you more comfortable talking with those in need than you would be otherwise.

You improve your skills through repetition and training. For a sufferer, most experiences of suffering are highly self-focused and limited. In serving others you increase your capacity to serve effectively by listening to lots of other stories and acquiring skills in that area.

One of our doctors, Linda, is a good example. She tells the story of an incident in a supermarket with a young woman dying of cancer.

> *I entered the supermarket and ran into Bob, an old friend. He was talking to a young woman named Mary, and after she moved on to shop, Bob told me quietly that she had three young kids and was actually dying of cancer.*

Later in an aisle I ran into her again. I said, non-intrusively, 'Mary, lovely to meet you, and can I say again how much we enjoyed the Rundell Primary School and I wish you all the best there. Bob did mention that you weren't well, so I wish you all the best with regard to that as well.'

She replied, 'Yes, I am dying of cancer.'

That led to a very intimate discussion, right there in the supermarket aisle, about how she was going, whether she had told her children and how were they going, whether her husband was getting partner support and whether they were all discussing it and facing it as a family. I thought, 'This is amazing—the most intimate sort of conversation that one can have with another person.' It made me deeply grateful that I had the relevant training and experience in how to talk to those who suffer.

Anonymous

Your life gains perspective that does not involve you. Suffering focuses your attention on yourself, but service can refocus your thoughts, helping you to stop looking in the mirror each day. I have found that service changes my perspective on life dramatically, driving me to ask 'how can I make a difference?' rather than 'how can I get more success?'

Service also recalibrates life. I used to worry about how my kids were doing at school until I saw kids who were suffering and dying. After that, I was totally happy with kids who were healthy and happy. It lifted me out of the trap of worrying about 'First World problems'.

You may receive thanks that warms your heart. Everybody I know who lives a life of compassionate service does it independent of any expression of gratitude. Indeed, they are often embarrassed when they win awards or receive expressions of thanks. They are not doing it for that reason.

But I have found personally, and I have seen for others, that gratitude really matters when you are struggling yourself and getting worn out. One of my colleagues, another disaster-relief team doctor, suffered a severe elbow infection after one of our trips. He ended up in the emergency department of his hospital and required ultrasound-guided drainage and intravenous antibiotics. This was undertaken by the head of the emergency department. Afterwards, my colleague emailed the doctor to thank him for his professionalism and kindness. The reply he got brought him to tears. The emergency doctor said he had been happy to help. 'In any case', he added, 'you were my inspiration as a medical student and have been my inspiration ever since.' What a gift at a time when my colleague was exhausted and sick.

How turning suffering into service can help others

If you have suffered, you have a unique way in which you can help others who have suffered or are suffering. To be helpful to someone you don't *need* to have suffered in the same way as them, but in some ways your experience and your story become your gift to them.

> *To suffer passes; to have suffered never passes.*
> *Anonymous French saying*

> *Your wound is your gift.*
> *Anonymous*

Service as an inspiration for others. The story is told of an old man who was asked by his grandson, 'Grandpa, at school we are told about people who have made the world a better place. What have you done in your life to do that?' I love that question. And I love the notion that we can choose to live our lives in a way that gives us an answer to any grandchild who asks it. Any reasonable response is unlikely to include wealth, power, fame or any of the other things that often capture our attention and tyrannise our lives. One ten-year-old girl wrote about her grandfather:

'Grandpa, what have you done in your life to help people and make the world a better place?'

> *My grandfather has a beautiful wife, three children and four grandchildren. He helps sick people and has received awards for his awesomeness. He inspires everyone around him to do good, in the name of Jesus. Mostly he inspires me to change the world.*
>
> *Anonymous*

A deeper reality lies behind this challenging question. When talking to the adult children of Christian parents and asking them why they dropped out of church and faith, the commonest answer is that it was irrelevant. To them their parents seemed indistinguishable from the non-Christian parents of their unchurched friends. Sacrificial, inspirational service (provided it does not erode rich family time) counters that. It can inspire children in a way that few other things can. While it will not be sufficient to make them Christians, it can counter the argument that you are selfish, safe, lazy and as egocentric as every other adult that they meet.

Service as ambassadorship. Whether we like it or not, we are Jesus' ambassadors in life. Personally I find ambassadorship a worry. I know I am flawed, distracted, lazy, selfish and many other things that make me an imperfect ambassador. But he has made us his ambassadors. Sacrificial service to those in need provides an opportunity to be a good ambassador rather than an absent or bad one.

> *We are therefore Christ's ambassadors, as though God were making his appeal through us.*
> *2 Corinthians 5:20*

Ambassadorship is not about proselytising—it is about showing the love of Jesus, reflecting his character. For example, our Christian team in fundamentalist Muslim Aceh was forbidden to mention Jesus or even sing songs in the evening. When I asked team members how they felt about that, they said they were happy to stay and serve, showing the compassion and love of Jesus by their actions. And impressive they were—performing sacrificial work at the coalface of the disaster, often in extremely difficult conditions.

I recently examined the leadership of a particular secular NGO and noticed that almost half of them were committed Christians. They were acting out of love, not with any other ulterior motive.

> *One of our HIV patients refused to allow me to speak with him for almost three months because of what he thought I represented—and understandably so. But over time he was willing to see me, and we got to know one another, talking mostly about his love of hunting and fishing. We never talked about God, never talked about faith, never opened the Bible—not once. But he believed that I was there for him, not for my own need to see another person 'get saved'.*
> *I didn't preach. I didn't quote a Scripture. I just needed to be present and to display the love of God to this man. Somehow God took over from there.*
> *Percy McCray[64]*

Service as an aroma. Christians are also Christ's 'aroma', and sacrificial service offers us a chance of being a sweet smell rather than a bad one. There is no doubt that being a sweet aroma of Jesus can have a powerful effect on others. In the words of one of St Francis's students, 'Preach the gospel, and when necessary use words.'

> *For we are to God the pleasing aroma of Christ among those who are being saved and those who are perishing.*
> *2 Corinthians 2:15*

Again I think of our team in Aceh. Anyone attempting to proselytise would have caused the whole team to be evicted from the province. But that did not mean the team left. Rather, they worked tirelessly in locations that many Western teams left alone because they were too difficult to get to and too uncomfortable to stay in. They also continued working well after other Western teams had packed up and gone home. Indeed, a year later they were still operating their clinics for the Acehnese people, like a beacon. Showing this kind of love unconditionally is a powerful reflection of the nature of God to those who suffer.

When asked for reasons for doing the work I do, I make no apologies for mentioning that my faith drives me. I make it clear that my service comes from my experience of God as a Christian, but also that this is just my story and I appreciate that other people perform compassionate service for other reasons. Mentioning my faith to me is like seeing a good movie or finding a good restaurant—it is natural to pass on the information. The listener can then take it or leave it. At a deeper level, I think of it more like the polio vaccine. If you know there is a good vaccine that can prevent polio, you want to tell people about it out of compassion.

> IF YOU KNOW THERE IS A GOOD VACCINE TO PREVENT
> POLIO YOU WANT TO TELL PEOPLE ABOUT IT

The pearl of great price is like that, and compassionate service, especially when it flows from personal suffering, provides a window of opportunity to explain that.

Examples of turning suffering into service

In chapter 8 I described some of the ways a horrendous circular-saw accident followed by months of excruciating pain changed my life—softening me as a person, increasing my empathy for others and embedding a sense of God's love in me in a profound way. That experience also led to different kinds of service. For example, it drove me to develop a special course for medical students around improving doctor-patient communication, something I have led for 25 years. It impacted on my willingness to show compassion to those suffering from natural disasters, resulting in serving as a volunteer doctor in Indonesia, Haiti and elsewhere. I also now regularly meet with old football friends to help them through the journey of cancer or other suffering.

Perhaps the most significant service that has come from my suffering is that it led to my becoming a better father. My near-death experience caused me to re-evaluate life's priorities, particularly the importance of time with family. I thank God for that wake-up call. I stopped going to work early and instead, once I was able, started walking with my son to school every day. I continued doing that for all the kids. I readjusted life's priorities, and I don't think I ever again lost sight of the importance of lots of special times with my children.

This also triggered me to write a book on fathering, *Dads and Their Daughters*, which became a bestseller and was the foundation for the formation of the award-winning 'The Fathering Project', which has established dads' groups in hundreds of schools in every state and has already helped hundreds of thousands of fathers become better dads and father figures. It has been described by one of Australia's former deputy prime ministers as 'the most powerful force in Australia to change the future of our kids'.

What follows are inspiring examples of Christians—some well known and some not—who have suffered then turned their suffering into service for others.

PETER LYNDON-JAMES: SERVING DRUG ADDICTS

His suffering. I first met Peter when he won a major award for community service. He is controversial because of his uncompromising approach, but to me he is a hero who is having more success on the scourge of methamphetamine addiction than anyone else.

Peter spent 26 years in institutions from the age of nine, graduating to adult prisons as a methamphetamine addict and pusher. He took drugs, used guns and hated his life. Then in gaol he started listening to a Christian radio station and felt it was speaking to him.

> *I remember when I was getting squished into the back of the police paddy wagon, screaming out to God, and I remembered a prayer that I learnt when I was a child about the shadow of death and fearing no evil. I passed out and I woke up in hospital the next day. I had a dream that God told me, 'Peter, after you get out of gaol again, are you gonna help people to change their lives?[65]'*

His service. Peter and his wife, Amanda, also a former methamphetamine user, started Shalom House, a drug rehabilitation centre in Perth founded on Christian principles. It caters for up to 140 men at a time. After two months of intensive support, those rehabilitating begin working in local businesses doing gardening, paving, plumbing, painting and other jobs. They learn decision-making, problem-solving and communication skills along with anger management.

Peter's past life inevitably affects him, but his work and dedication are inspirational. Shalom House has a very high success rate and a waiting list for admission.

CHAD VARAH: SERVING THE MENTALLY ILL

His suffering. An Anglican priest, Chad was impacted during one of his early parish appointments when a teenage girl committed suicide. As he sat and talked with her parents during the funeral, he was deeply saddened. He became more concerned about the mental suffering of members of his parish and community and offered counselling. But he wanted to do something more specific to help people contemplating suicide.

His service. By 1953 he had moved to London where placed a notice in the newspaper inviting anyone who was at risk of suicide to phone him.

> *I made my debut in the ministry by burying a 14-year-old girl who had killed herself when her periods started, thinking she was ill. Then I read that there were three suicides a day in Greater London, and I realised there ought to be an emergency number for suicidal people[66].*

He was inundated, and soon volunteers joined him to help. This was the beginning of the hugely successful, international Samaritans crisis phone line, which today has over 20,000 volunteers and 201 branches in the UK and Ireland alone.

When he started, Varah said he was just 'a man willing to listen, with a base and an emergency telephone'. The power of volunteers—to listen, confidentially and without judgment—turned out to be the real strength of the service.

PETER PROUT: FROM EMOTIONAL ABUSE TO MENTOR AND TEACHER

His suffering: From the time he started school, Peter was bullied by his farmer father, a ferociously angry man who was quick to punish any mistake, physically and emotionally. Terrified of his dad, Peter ran away from home at 15. He ended up in the Australian army and was nearly killed during fighting in Borneo in 1965–66. He was helicoptered out and spent a year in hospital recovering.

His service: One day when sitting on a tractor, Peter became aware, out of the blue, of God's presence, and the sense of a voice saying, 'You are OK. This is not all there is for you. There will be better for you. I love you, and you are OK.' After leaving the army he obtained a degree in education, then a doctorate and further training in Canada and the USA. He returned to be a prominent teacher, award-winning lecturer in education, and mentor and 'father figure' to thousands of young people.

JONI EARECKSON TADA: SERVING THE DISABLED

Her suffering: At age 17 Joni Eareckson Tada dove into the Chesapeake Bay, crunched her head against the bottom and became a quadriplegic. During her rehabilitation she experienced anger, depression and suicidal thoughts. .

> *I ignored the verses... in which Jesus teaches that forgiving sin is a lot harder to do than healing someone. I didn't care about that teaching. Forget the sin part; I just wanted the healing part... I felt bewildered and utterly lost... The despair was claustrophobic, and I finally whimpered, 'I can't live this way. I'm so lost. God, show me how to live.' It was my first plea for help[67].*

Her service: Joni's 1976 autobiography, *Joni: An Unforgettable Story*, became an international bestseller. In 1979 she established Joni and Friends, an organization dedicated to supporting people with disabilities and their families. The Joni and Friends International Disability Center now runs programs ranging from retreats for families affected by disability to Wheels for the World, which collects wheelchairs and other mobility devices for developing nations. She served on the National Council on Disability under Presidents Reagan and Bush and has advised the US State Department and many other bodies. Author of over 50 books, singer, broadcaster and conference speaker, she is recognised internationally as an advocate for people with disabilities.

> *I know this: I'm in the zone whenever I infuse Christ-encouragement into the hearts of people like Tommy [a quadriplegic]... It feels so right to agonize alongside them... I really would rather be in this wheelchair knowing Jesus as I do than be on my feet without him[68].*

ELISABETH ELLIOT: SERVING OVERSEAS IN FORGIVENESS

Her suffering: Elisabeth's first husband, Jim Elliot, was speared to death, along with four missionary friends, while attempting to make contact with the Auca Indians in Ecuador. They had a ten-month-old daughter, Valerie, at the time.

> *Five days later I knew that Jim was dead. And God's presence with me was not Jim's presence. That was a terrible fact. God's presence didn't change the terrible fact that I was now a widow, and I expected to be a widow until I died[69].*

Her service: Some years later, Elisabeth returned to work amongst the same tribe that killed her husband. She went on to write over 20 widely read books including *Your Suffering Is* Never *for Nothing, A Path Through Suffering: Discovering the Relationship Between God's Mercy and Our Pain* and *The Path of Loneliness: Finding Your Way Through the Wilderness to God*. Through these and a radio program, 'Gateway to Joy', she helped hundreds of thousands of people.

FLORENCE NIGHTINGALE: SERVING THE SICK

Her suffering: As a young Christian woman, Florence went in 1854 to serve as a nurse in the grue- some Crimean War. She found mouldy food, scarce water, filth, overcrowding, no sanitary arrange- ments, no bedsheets, no operating tables, no medical supplies. She collapsed from overwork and returned home gaunt and pale.

Her service: When the war ended, she was the sole hero to emerge. Queen Victoria presented her with a diamond brooch. She went on to be the best-known nurse in history, consulted by royalty and even by the US president. She established schools for training nurses and introduced procedures that have been benefiting people ever since.

> *I think one's feelings waste themselves in words, they ought all to be distilled into actions and into actions which bring results*[70].

JOHN NEWTON: FROM SUICIDE AND SLAVE TRADING TO 'AMAZING GRACE'

His suffering: John's mother died when he was six, and in 1743, at the age of 18, he was forcibly pressed into England's Royal Navy. He was flogged after trying to desert and later enslaved in West Africa. At one stage he contemplated suicide. After being rescued, his ship came close to sinking in a storm. He then became a slave trader for nine years.

His service: After converting to Christianity, Newton served as an Anglican minister in several parishes in England. When he was in London, one of his stepchildren had a mental breakdown and was interred in Bethlem Royal Hospital in east London, one of the first 'insane asylums', infamous for practices including starvation and beatings. He was not allowed to visit her, but every day he would walk to the hospital, stand on the pavement outside her room and wave so she knew he was 'there for her'. He became an abolitionist, mentored William Wilberforce and actively campaigned for an end to the slave trade. He also wrote the hymn 'Amazing Grace'.

HENRY DUNANT: SERVING THE WOUNDED IN BATTLE (THE RED CROSS)

His suffering: Henry was a young Swiss Christian from a middle-class family who founded the 'Thursday Association', a loose band of young men that met to study the Bible and help the poor. In 1852 they helped create the Young Men's Christian Association (YMCA) in 1852. Seven years later Henry came upon the scene of a bloody battle in Italy where 40,000 men lay dead or dying on the battlefield without medical attention.

His service: On the battlefield Henry organised local people to tend to the fallen. After returning to Geneva, he called for the creation of national relief societies to assist those wounded in war. This led to the setting up in 1863 of an International Committee for Relief to the Wounded, which later became the International Committee of the Red Cross and led to the framing of the first Geneva Convention. He was awarded the Nobel Peace Prize for this work in 1901.

Temper your passion to serve with a clear view of God's priorities

Another person who made a big difference by turning suffering into service was Bob Pierce, the founder of World Vision. But Bob's story also sounds a note of caution.

 Bob was visiting a relief agency in Korea when he saw an abandoned little girl and was asked the probing question, 'What are you going to do about her?' The agency could not afford to care for her. He was deeply moved, gave some money and began photographing Asian orphans to raise funds for them in America. His heart and photos touched people and soon the agency World Vision was born. He later started a second Christian relief agency, Samaritan's Purse.

But Bob was an almost completely absent father and husband. His daughter Sharon telephoned him once, told him how depressed she was and asked if somehow he could come home and spend some time with her. He didn't. Sharon's mother found her daughter in the hospital with her wrists bandaged—she had tried to take her own life. She said, 'I just needed to feel Daddy's arms around me.'

Bob's passion for service and ministry was noble and wonderfully effective. But he allowed it to deflect him from the family responsibilities that God had given him. Indeed, strong family relationships are usually a foundation for effective ministry—I have certainly found that.

Great suffering can create great passion for service, but Bob's tale is a cautionary one about not allowing that passion to damage your family in the process.

DON'T BE DISTRACTED BY UNREASONABLE CRITICISM

It is fair to say that compassionate service can run into headwinds. Criticism can call into question your sincere efforts to show compassion to others.

When that happens, the first thing is to ask, Are these criticisms reasonable? For example, are you neglecting your family in your service? Are you failing to collaborate with others who are doing similar sorts of service? Are you serving in a way that is not Christian? Are you failing to plan—to count the cost before 'building the tower'?

But there are other ways you can receive criticism that have nothing to do with how you are showing love to others in service. Possibly your service reminds others of their lack of service and makes them feel bad about themselves, and they can react accordingly. Some forms of response can be egocentric (for example, parents who don't want their adult children to go to the mission field because they will miss their grandchildren).

> IT IS BETTER TO LIGHT A CANDLE
> THAN TO CURSE THE DARKNESS

Still others challenge service on pragmatic grounds: 'There are so many millions suffering—what can one person do?' As a scientist, I often undertake that analysis myself. But I am still profoundly influenced by a phrase I heard when I was a young doctor: 'It is better to light a candle than to curse the darkness.'

A Holy Spirit-softened heart

I encourage you to consider, then, once you are able, turning your personal suffering into compassionate service to others. This chapter has described the often-spectacular benefits of doing that. Making a big difference is possible.

Yet it is not fundamentally about making a difference. It is about responding to the compassion you feel in your heart, a heart softened by the Holy Spirit, to turn your own personal suffering into compassionate care for others. That will involve a cost, it will involve taking risks, and it may involve swimming against the current of criticism. But it will also embody the Christian understanding of 'growth through suffering'—in this case, growth through service that enables others to grow.

> *Learn to do good; seek justice, correct oppression; bring justice to the fatherless, plead the widow's cause.*
> *Isaiah 1:17 (ESV)*

> *Twenty years from now you will be more disappointed by the things you didn't do than by the ones you did. So throw off the bowlines, sail away from the safe harbor, catch the trade winds in your sails. Explore. Dream. Discover.*
> **Sarah Frances Brown**[71]

> *If the highest aim of a captain were to preserve his ship, he would keep it in port.*
> **Thomas Aquinas**[72]

I hope you find this chapter an encouragement to turn suffering, either as a victim or carer, into service to others. Those who have done so have transformed their suffering into a Jesus-like compassion that not only gives meaning to that personal suffering but also prevents or responds to the suffering of others in beautiful ways.

Key points

- Turning suffering into service benefits both those who are served and those who have suffered.
- Turning suffering into service is a choice.
- Jesus' story of the Good Samaritan is at the heart of compassionate service.
- Use the gifts and opportunities you already have to serve—your experience of suffering might be one of them.
- Accept that serving requires some risk and some costs.
- Turning suffering into service is good ambassadorship and spreads the sweet aroma of Jesus.
- Stay focused on God's priorities for you along with your passion to serve.

Postscript

In this book I have tried to look at suffering from 'behind the tears', from the point of view of the sufferer and of those who seek to care for them well. As a doctor 'at the coalface', I felt I needed to write a book that addressed the huge questions of suffering I am asked most often: Why is this suffering happening? How can I handle it?

I have shared insights and strategies that flow from my coalface experience. I have also shared my conviction that the Bible is clear that suffering is not meant to leave us in a valley of despair but to transform us, to make us better people.

That conviction is confirmed by personal experience, both my own and others'. I have shared the experiences of many here—they have helped me improve in my ability to respond to suffering with insight and empathy. I have also tried to be honest in disclosing my own personal suffering. How honest are you about your personal suffering? Do you discuss these things with friends and family? I hope this book helps you become more open about your own journey with suffering. If a private person like me can do this, anyone can.

If I were asked about the outcomes I would like to see from this book, I would reply that I would love to see the following:

For those who are suffering, I would love to see them read the book early in their journey and accept three things: (1) that there is no crystal-clear answer to the 'why' question, (2) that they should not blame themselves and (3) that suffering is, annoyingly, a promised part of the Christian journey because that is how we grow best. And when these facts make the sufferer angry (which they mostly will), I hope they will feel freer to express their anger and frustration at God, because he wants them to. Of course, being prepared in this way won't stop any sufferer feeling sad and angry, but it means they won't be surprised.

I hope too that each person who suffers will embrace the daily Diamond Meditation described in chapter 3, or some similar form of biblical reflection that keeps them from being locked in a prison of bitterness.

Ultimately, I would love to see sufferers softened in heart and wiser in head because of their suffering, rejoicing at how they have grown and turning that suffering into service of others. If their suffering involves death (for example, terminal cancer), I would love to see them 'die well and not badly', talking openly and honestly with their families and friends, laughing and crying with them, getting closure on their life and encouraging their family to honour them by 'paying forward' any good thing they have learnt from the person who is dying.

For those who are close to people who are suffering, I would love to see them learn how to listen, empathise, act helpfully and pray appropriately, avoiding the minefield of unhelpful words and actions that, despite good intentions, so often make it harder for sufferers. I would love to see family members and friends also grow and learn from the experience, and, as the Bible intends, turn it into compassionate care for others. My vision is of church communities and pastors who have learnt how to do these things so well that any person in the congregation who suffers can feel confident that they will experience compassion from others and will feel free to be honest about how they are travelling.

From my personal point of view, my hope is that my many experiences of suffering will help others understand, survive and grow from their own suffering. I found it hard to write this book—apart from the time it took in an already busy life, I was continually worried that the deep issues discussed could only be summarised, and I could 'feel' the frustration of the reader because of that. That is why the 'huggy bear' appears so often. But in the end, if just one person or family benefits from this book, it will have been a worthwhile effort.

References and additional resources are listed at:
https://www.brucerobinson.com.au/personal/suffering.

Printed in Australia
AUHW022004041122
371151AU00005B/5